Janner on
Pitching for Business

GREVILLE JANNER

Janner on Pitching for Business

A complete guide to
winning beauty contests in business

HUTCHINSON BUSINESS BOOKS LIMITED

First published in Great Britain in 1990 by
Hutchinson Business Books Limited
An imprint of Random Century Limited
20 Vauxhall Bridge Road, London SW1V 2SA

Random Century Australia (Pty) Limited
20 Alfred Street, Milsons Point, Sydney
New South Wales 2061, Australia

Random Century New Zealand Limited
9–11 Rothwell Avenue, Albany
Private Bag, North Shore Mail Centre
Glenfield, Auckland 10, New Zealand

Century Hutchinson South Africa (Pty) Limited
PO Box 337, Bergvlei 2012, South Africa

Photoset in Times 10/12 by Deltatype Ltd, Ellesmere Port
Printed and bound in Great Britain by
Mackays of Chatham PLC, Chatham, Kent

British Library Cataloguing in Publication Data

Janner, Greville
    Janner on pitching for business: a complete guide to winning
        beauty contests in business.
    I. Business firms. Competition
    I. Title
    338.6048

ISBN 0–09–174544–6
ISBN 0–09–174545–4 pbk

For CYRIL STEIN
with admiration, affection and respect

Contents

Part III   DOCUMENTATION AND VISUAL AIDS

Part IV   TECHNIQUES AT THE PITCH – HOW TO WIN

Part V   SPECIAL TARGET OCCASIONS AND AUDIENCES

Part VI   THE LAW

Part VII   THE FOLLOW UP AND THE END

Introduction

Winning business against competition means beating your competitors. To do that, you must study, practise and excel at the art of 'pitching' – often in what are now known as 'beauty contests' or 'beauty parades'.

While at one time you could perhaps have sat back and waited for business to flow in to you, today you must go out and get it. That means convincing prospective customers or clients that your products or services or both are better, more cost-effective and more attractive than those offered by your competitors.

Cost and quality are, of course, still crucial. But the less the difference between yours and those of your competitors, the more personal or individual the service which you are offering must appear to be. To win, you must present your company, your product or service and – always – yourself, to best effect.

This book reveals the secrets of winning 'beauty contests'. It contains the techniques which we have studied and practised and errors which we teach our clients. It covers everything from preparation to choosing, rehearsing and knitting together your team and understanding and using visual aids with skill and economy – plus some essential law, from contracts to corruption.

We look at documentation – how to match the style of your documents to your message and your image. And we consider basic presentational skills within the context of the beauty contest – not only for when you yourself are speaking, but also for when you or your colleagues are meant to be listening!

In every beauty contest there is, of course, an important element of chemistry, which you may to some extent adjust. There is also an element of luck: some you will win, some you may lose, but you will certainly win more if you follow the rules in this book. For those you lose, we have some suggestions for lifting yourself gingerly off the canvas and back into the ring.

You may think that politics is an unpleasant business, only indulged in by politicians. 'A statesman' goes the classic definition, 'is a dead politician!' Well, a non-political businessperson is a dead entrepreneur. There is as much politics in business life as at Westminster or in local authorities. Winning competitive pitches demands political acumen, skill and cunning, and we show you how to develop and use your political skills. Every competition – from childhood examinations to parliamentary elections, from major business beauty parades and pitches, to private gatherings or one-to-one efforts to win orders or arguments – requires courage, determination and methodology. In these pages, I will explain something of the psychology and tactics of the hunt.

Finally, a word about terminology. How should I describe the people who go pitching, and their prospective clients and customers? The word 'pitchers' seems more suitable for biblical water carrying, and 'prospective clients or customers' is clumsy. So, as often as not, the pitchers become 'you', and the people whose work you are trying to win your 'quarry' or 'judges'. The truth is that you are the hunter: you have (or you should have) your prospect in sight – even though in the world of the beauty contest, it is technically your quarry who are hunting you! They are your judges.

I would like to thank all those who have – consciously or unconsciously – taught me the rules, tricks and techniques of pitching. They include generations of professional and business people to whom my colleagues and I have taught presentational skills in general and competitive pitching techniques in particular.

To my daughter, Laura Janner-Klausner, my thanks for helping to prepare and edit this and all my other books. To Leslie Benson, my thanks for your assistance.

And to you who will use these techniques to win – I wish you success, beyond even that which you will deserve!

Greville Janner QC MP

Part I

SHORT LISTS, PREPARATION, REHEARSALS AND THE FOUR QUESTIONS

1

The Short List and Retaining your Client

'Critics', said one of them, 'always want to put you into pigeon holes, which are very uncomfortable unless you happen to be a pigeon!'

Actors have a horror of stereotyping. The comedian wants a lead in a Shakespeare tragedy, the tragedian, a comic role.

In the world of pitching, you want to play to your strength – which may not be the same as that perceived by potential employers. If it is, you are lucky and your reputation may carry you onto the shortlist. If not, then you must battle for the privilege of pitching.

Selecting a shortlist for *commercial* beauty parades is not that different from the same process in the real ones: contestants are selected by reputation, by recommendation or by elimination. Personal contact, unsolicited mailshots or an appropriate register create the first list. Among the reasons for getting on the short list are:

- Record and renown in the sector – a good name goes beyond price.
- Understanding of clients' requirements – of both product and services.
- Reputation or previous contact with the principals ('The devil they know . . .') including special skills.
- Relevant offers – which will depend entirely on the nature of the pitch. Examples from the advertising world are sales promotion, direct marketing, public relations and design services. You can soon identify the equivalent in your territory.
- Attitude towards client – including enthusiasm for the job.

To get on to the shortlist, you must work out what your potential clients want. Are you providing the needs from your current, known, perceived excellence? Or are you stereotyped into an area which you would do well to ease yourself out of? How can you raise your profile in those areas where you have the desire and the ability to expand?

In athletics, you do not get into the final until you have won the heats. The problem with pitching is that the heats are often invisible, and you may not know of the final until someone else has won it.

So look over the routes to that shortlist and do all you can to make yourselves visible and desirable to those who will select. Many would wish to pitch but few are chosen. To be amongst them is the first essential.

Of course, the best way to make a living is by satisfying and retaining the clients or customers you already have. The next best is by responding to people with a known interest. Only third come the direct mail or other trawling operations which may, if you are lucky, put you onto the shortlist for a pitch.

Most pitches are expected and intentional. You can prepare for them because you recognize them for what they are. Others are potentially more lethal because you would not recognize them – and that includes informal presentations to people who visit your premises.

It follows that you should learn to recognize a pitch when you are or should be making one. Do not be fooled by informality, whether yours or anyone else's. Treat a pitching occasion on your own premises with the same respect as you would do if it were on anyone else's. As with impromptu speeches, unexpected pitches soon sort out the professionals from the amateurs, the trained from the unskilled.

2

Preparation – Step by Step

If you are planning a new product or service, you know that if you follow a disciplined routine, you will – at least in the long run – save resources and increase your efficiency. The same applies to preparing for pitching.

To plan your pitch, sit down with the colleagues who will be most involved in and affected by it. This includes those who, if you succeed, will do the work for and with the clients, and those who are in charge of that area of your activity, even if they may not take part in the pitch or in an eventual operation.

Pads and pens ready, you can now 'brainstorm' for answers to the following questions:

Who are *they*? Identify and target the quarry.

What do they want?

What do *you* want to achieve – what are you selling?

Who are your *competitors*? If you do not know, try to find out. If your quarry declines to tell you, can you find out by some side route?

What are *our* advantages and disadvantages and what are *theirs*? Examine your own outfit and resources with total frankness.

The final question is '*how*?' How do you maximize your advantages in the eyes of your prospective clients? Then reverse the question: How can we make the most of their disadvantages, while at the same time building on our own assets?

Part of the solution may lie in the answer to the next question: What team should you field? Who should be included and who left out? What level will the other side deploy and who should respond? What areas should the team cover, and who should deal with each? How long have you got in total for your pitch? How much have you been asked to – or anyway, how much should you – allocate to answering questions? How long should you allocate to each participant?

Finally, take a preliminary look at the sort of documentation and visual aids you are likely to need. Make no irreversible decisions, but take a preliminary view.

Of course, all this takes time. When it's done, pause. At best, go away and think about it, at least overnight. Let the team's minds tick over, and they will come up with new ideas and inspiration. Participants should prepare their own individual presentations and contributions. Where appropriate, they should sketch out the documentation and visual aids which they will each use.

All the above should be done with outside or inside help. Harness independent minds and experience as and when you can; try to put yourself in the eyes, minds and places of those who will judge. It is precisely because it is easier for others to judge the effect which you will have on third parties that you should bring outsiders in, if you can. Otherwise, try to bring in at least one insider, who is sufficiently detached to look out.

In *Thinking on Your Feet*, Louis Nizer declared: 'Preparation is the be-all of good trial work. Everything else – felicity of expression, improvizational brilliance – is a satellite around the sun. Thorough preparation is that sun.' He was right.

3

Who Leads?

Top leaders win. The leader of a pitching team organizes, supervises and criticizes the preparation, and chairs, controls, co-ordinates and fronts the presentation. If you have the wrong leader or the leader gets it wrong, you are in trouble.

The best leaders are chosen by their team. They are obviously outstanding, their talents are recognized and accepted, and they lead by consent. They listen.

So when choosing your team, start with the leader. To follow your leader is only easy and successful if you get the right one.

Beauty contest leaders must themselves be at least adequate presenters. They should be able to put a case to maximum effect, or at least to understand how to draw together others who will do so. If they cannot put the case, they must at least be able to summarize it.

Like captains of ships, leaders must know how to navigate. Like successful heads of businesses, they must know how to judge, and recognize that their set-up will be judged by their skill and standing.

They must know how to Chair – and how to control from the Chair. For instance, it is for them to make sure that their teams do not argue and dispute amongst themselves when they are in front of their quarry and surrounded by other hunters.

You may feel that your MD, senior partner or other top executive is the natural choice to pitch for a particular contract, but you must make an objective assessment of his or her assets and liabilities in the particular circumstances of the contest in view. Ask yourself:

- Will the best individual be readily available – enthusiastic to take on the job – or be too tied up to prepare it adequately?
- Which person will be most acceptable to your team and to the judges?
- Is this one of those rare cases where someone who would not normally be the best person for the job will fit into it for some

special reason – such as specialist knowledge or a friendship with the individual who will make the choice?

The qualities of the particular leader will depend on circumstances, but the job of a leader must be to sit in the centre, to bring out the best of the team and, once out front, to take control and command.

4

Preparing and Resourcing Preparation

As competition increases, so does the effort and expense lavished on a tender, estimate or quotation, in the form of draughtsmen, printers, etc. The product is then handed over to the presenters – who may promptly squander the entire investment with an ill-conceived, under-prepared, poorly thrown together presentation. So, always:

- Budget presentations in terms of preparation, documentation, visual aids, presenters' time, etc.
- Compare the resources spared for a proposal, quotation, estimate or tender, as against those spared for the presentation itself – training, preparation, rehearsal, documentation, visual aids, presenters' time, etc.

If you increased your expenditure on the presentation by 50 per cent, what percentage would that add to the overall cost of the effort to win the contract? Would your chances of success be increased by a far higher percentage? For instance:

- How many of your presenters are properly trained for that crucial function? Is your Chair, managing director or chief executive a superb technician, administrator, businessperson – but a poor presenter and either unwilling to admit inadequacy or unprepared to learn?
- Do you or your colleagues underestimate the need for skill in selling? Do your subordinates say of you (as so many complain to us about their bosses), 'We can get him to attend the proposal meeting, but not to learn how not to mess up his part in the operation'? Are they unwilling to tell you the truth about your poor performance because you hold their prospects in your hands?
- Have you enquired whether you might be one of those top

people who ruins their colleagues' presentation because, although a genius at your job, you are unprepared, untutored and unsophisticated in the art and craft of the presenter? What would it cost to put this right?

If the answer to any of these questions is unsatisfactory, then join the club of commercial wasters – people who spend freely on preparation of estimates, tenders and quotations, but little or nothing on the crucial presentations that will decide whether or not the rest of their effort is thrown away. There are certain nations, well-known in the world of international politics and bluster, which spend imperial fortunes on armaments, including the most sophisticated aircraft and other weapons. But when it comes to war, they do not possess the trained and motivated manpower, skilled and able to put the hardware to its devastating purpose. You could lose business as they lose wars.

5

Predestination – Are You in with a Chance?

There are some pitches you can't win. It's all a formality: the dice are pre-loaded, the outcome predetermined, the whole contest an unreality. So how can you spot a sham in advance? If you do, is it worth investing your resources in a hopeless fight? And if so, how can you create at least a chance of success? If it is all decided in advance, why should the hosts waste their time putting on beauty contests at all?

The answer is, probably, for 'show': to give the impression that they have an open mind and are looking for the best. Then why should they not take the best when they find it? Maybe because they are already satisfied with what they have. Or maybe the predeter-mined winners are friends of (say) the chief executive.

You should, in any event, be doing your best to beam in on your prospect, trying to find out what they really want and who holds the butter, and it is via this route that you may spot the 'predetermined'. Can you find an inside contact who will tell you the real truth about your prospects?

We once sought a contract to teach presentational skills to a major company. The director in charge of training was the decision-maker and the training manager made the arrangements. This training manager resented the director and, in the course of some mild chatting up, told us the sad truth – that the boss had already made up his mind to continue with the people they already had. Worse: the beauty contest had been laid on because the Chairman knew us and said we should be given a chance, which the training director thought was a waste of time and which he thoroughly resented!

We fought – and, of course, we lost. But when I next saw the Chairman, I did drop the lightest of hints about the reality of the contest and we did end by training him personally.

We don't believe in backing out of beauty contests. If we know that the dice are pre-loaded, we still put on the best show we can. Perhaps the predestined winners will go bust or fall out with their clients. Or maybe the director will leave, the butter will melt and we will fit their new mould. There is no certainty, even with beauty contests fixed in advance. No wise lawyer will ever tell a client, 'you're bound to win'. In elections, you do not over-estimate the polls. You count votes after they are in the ballot box – until then, you fight for them. So with beauty contests: you have not lost until someone else has been announced as the winner. Until then, there is only one certainty – that if you do not take part, you have no chance of winning.

Not to enter a beauty contest because you fear defeat is a form of advance resignation. You never know your luck until you try it. Morality apart, your only deterrent must be the amount of resources which you would like to commit to an enterprise which you are more likely to lose than most.

6

No Time to Prepare

There are two reasons why you may get pitched into pitching, unprepared. First, you may simply feel that you don't have time for preparation. Second, the prospect may telephone and say 'We'd love to see you – today, please.'

The first reason is a bad one. Busy people make time: if you can't, then you must go into battle ill–equipped, knowing that your prospects of victory are greatly reduced. A top US trainer told me: 'We reckon that 75 per cent of your winning is done before you reach the battleground.' An exaggeration perhaps, but essentially correct – bad planning paves the road to losing. Apart from any other consideration, you are reducing your own confidence. And as you are, above all, selling your own confidence, you should build it by preparing.

Regard each pitch as you would have done an important examination at a school or university. If you have to swot up late into the night before, that's too bad. Exams begin many long nights before the grim moment arrives.

If prospective clients or customers leave you with no option, then take some extra deep breaths, use every moment available, flip through your Four Questions – and go for it. Get your staff and researchers on the trail and harness every second you have.

When you arrive, don't apologize – they'll know you were only called about the meeting minutes or hours before. Instead, be positive. Thank them for giving you the chance to offer your services or products, however late in the day. Emphasize that you are a bright, disciplined team, ready to tackle the unexpected, the swift opportunity, the unexpected emergency.

If you've got even an hour to prepare, that's not 'impromptu'. You've got time to do your 'P. . .R. . .E. . .P': to work out the *Proposition* you are seeking to sell; the best *Reason* for buying it; an *example* or two; then to beam in again on the *Proposition*, straight onto your prospective clients or customers.

You have time to jot down your ideas on your cards, your theme (saying what you are going to say), your main points, and the order – which you can shuffle, along with the cards (saying it), plus your final message (saying what you have said).

The unexpected opportunity, then, may provide precisely the chance you need, to prove your worth and to snatch a new opportunity from those better warned.

Finally, a horror story, told to us by clients. Ill-advised by a PR company, they prepared a major, slick, presentation for what they had been told would be a full board turnout of some 15 people.

They found to their dismay that there were only two, but put on the whole of their prepared presentation, standing embarrassed and uncomfortable. Of course, they lost the job, and the PR company a client.

7

Rehearsals

'Rehearsing a play,' said playwright Peter Shaffer, 'is making the word into flesh. Publishing a play is reversing the process.' Rehearsing a pitch is making plans live. Rehearse carefully and the pitch itself will not reverse that process. Or as the famous magician, Harry Blackstone, put it: 'Nothing I do can't be done by a ten-year-old . . . with 15 years of practice'.

Practice makes pitches. The first rehearsal should be a relaxed but careful brainstorming run-through. Jot down all your main points and decide whether these should go into opening statements, and if so, then by whom. Should some of them be left for question time, knowing or hoping that they will be asked, or at least confident that if they are not, you can tackle them with confidence?

Next, go away and mull over your decisions and arrangements and, not least, your own contribution. You will inevitably come up with new ideas. Put them to your colleagues – and prepare for the *dress rehearsal*.

This second rehearsal is crucial. Spare time for it. Make sure that all the cast turn up. Kick around any new ideas and slot the presentation into place. Then rehearse it, preferably to independent minds, already within or brought in from outside. If possible, record the session on video so that you can see what you look like, both on and off stage.

With the help of your critics, assess the impact of your presentation. With the help of your audio-visual equipment, watch and listen and criticize yourselves. Learn from and help improve each other.

Finally, leave time for a question and answer session. Rehearse, discuss and decide on the best answers to the trickiest questions. This will have two results:

● Knowing that you have the answers ready, you will not only *be* but also *feel* prepared. This will give you confidence, which you will show. It will also help you with your nerves.

- When the questions come, you will deal with them professionally. If they do not, what have you lost? A little of your time, nothing more.

A major firm of solicitors recently decided to take on PR consultants. They invited four top firms to present their work. The senior partner told me: 'All the firms were well recommended, professional and successful. That's why we invited them to pitch. Everything depended on their presentations. Being PR outfits, we expected them all to be first class. They weren't.

'Two of the presentations were a total disaster, one or more of the team being inarticulate and the whole presentation being the sort of mess that they would never allow their own clients to produce, we hoped. Certainly we were not going to give them the chance to experiment on us.

'The third was pretty ordinary. Straightforward, well thought out, but essentially boring. No spark. No chemistry with us.

'Only one really came to life, relaxed and related to our needs. OK, so we knew that they had done research and had rehearsed their pitch. It was a well-produced presentation – but that told us what they would also be prepared to do for us. They got the job.'

8

Pausing and Silence

The best story on the effectiveness of pausing was told of the famous lawyer, F E Smith, the First Earl of Birkenhead. While he was a young undergraduate at Oxford, a famous don invited him for a stroll. The academic used a well-known trick – he would leave it to the student to start the conversation. After a long silence, the student would make some in-consequential remark and the don would crush him with his reply.

F E Smith worked out his own plan of action. He walked alongside the don in complete silence for over an hour. Finally, the don felt embarrassed and said, 'They tell me that you are clever, Smith. Is that right?' 'Yes,' replied Mr Smith.

Silence resumed until they were back in the College. 'Goodbye, sir,' said Smith, 'I have greatly enjoyed our talk.'

More silence means greater success.

When we taught our children how not to get knocked down when crossing the road, we used the classic road safety slogan: 'Stop! Look! Listen!' To assess your presentation before you make it, use the same method.

'Stop!' means don't rush. As I was taught in the Army, 'Softly, softly, catchee monkee', or, to use the classic Latin tag, *festina lente* – hasten slowly. Pause to assess your performance, then decide where it can be improved.

The best way to 'Look!' is with audio-visual equipment: a simple combination of camera and screen will let you see your performance. From the tape, you will note your team's faults, such as:

- Speakers slouching, looking unconfident or incompetent.
- Eyes up, down, or swivelling sideways.
- Inadequate visual aids – or visual aids unprofessionally, clumsily used.
- Non-speakers not attending – looking at their own notes,

worrying about their own contributions, or simply looking quizzical, cynical or bored.

You could 'Listen!' with a tape recorder, or play back your audio tape without the vision. Until you get used to hearing your own voice, don't be surprised if it sounds unrecognizable. Don't forget, you usually hear it from inside your head.

Do you sound sincere and convincing or are you gabbling, slurring your words, dropping your voice at the end of sentences? And what about your colleagues?

To stand back and evaluate yourself is not easy: some people cannot recognize the blemishes in their own performances. They may be the result of self-love. When once asked whether he was enjoying himself, Bernard Shaw replied 'Indeed I am, there's nothing else here to enjoy!' Others are too hard on themselves, too critical, or too depressed about their own skills.

Always try to bring in outside observers. The more important the pitch, the more crucial its outcome, the more help you need. Once again, look for someone within your organization experienced in pitches and not afraid to criticize. Or use outsiders. One of the most frequent and fascinating jobs that we do for our clients is to whisk them through rehearsals. Constructive criticism in advance is far better than miserable post mortems, following costly failures.

Rehearsal training is not as easy as it may appear. For instance, if people are coming up to a major pitch, you must build and not destroy their confidence. That often means putting up with individual presentation faults which more leisurely training could have cured. You must make the best of the clay mould, within the time you have.

9

Judging

To judge yourself is always a problem. Remember those exams where you thought that you had excelled, but when the results came through, you found that your examiners had not recognized your brilliance? Conversely, what of those times when you emerged from the exam room, depressed and wretched, convinced that you had failed – and the results were triumphant?

The best time to judge a performance is at the rehearsal, and the finest judges of your public presentations are your family. They'll soon tell you how you did. You won't even need to ask – just look at their faces.

It follows that the next time you hear that your own outfit is putting on a beauty contest, you should sit in on it. At best, put yourself onto the panel that chooses. At worst, sit in, take notes and then discuss the results with the judges.

Now put yourself into the judges' shoes. How will you weigh the competitors?

Reputation
You will start from the base of the reputation of your competitors. What have they actually achieved in the past? Never mind the promises, how reliable have they proved themselves in practice? What is their record of service for you or for others?

You may, of course, know the answers from your own experience of them, or from their references or recommendations. Otherwise, you must look to the evidence they lay before you – including their client lists, their documentation, slides or whatever else they may show you.

Authority
Reputation lays a firm basis for authority. The odds are, though, that the pitchers will all have good past records, or they would not

be on the list of possibles for the future – which means that you must assess the individuals before you. At this stage, it is their individual presentational skills – or lack of them – which will count. For instance, does their posture and other body language show confidence in themselves and their abilities? Do they look you in the eyes when they make their assertions, or are their bodies slumped and their eyes shifty? Do you trust them?

Like any other judge, in court or in commerce, you must learn to discriminate between truth and untruth. You must decide whether or not you like and trust the individuals and whether you would place your confidence and your orders and contacts with them.

Money

Cash counts, but not for everything. You will decide what you are prepared to spend and how best to spend it. You will look for the least expensive – but in doing so, you should look at the long as well as at the short run. You will seek people who are effective and products that are cost-effective.

You will also look most carefully at competitors' costings and will test them, both from your own knowledge and with expert advice, and through questioning of the pitchers.

People

You will want to know who will actually, physically handle your business. Which individuals? It's not enough to rely on the business – the larger the outfit, the more important it becomes to know who will actually be looking after you and yours. Is that individual taking part in the pitch? If so, then is the chemistry right? If not, then why not?

As with individual interviews, so with a pitch – which is really nothing more than a group interview. Chemistry counts.

When you literally put yourself into the place of the judges, your perception changes. By judging others, you get a new view of yourselves. Ask yourself: will we satisfy their needs and how can *we* convince *them*?

Tape Recorders, Dictating Machines and Preparation

Sir Winston Churchill and great actors may succeed in making written English sound splendid when spoken. For the rest of us, there are only two alternatives: either presentations must be genuinely impromptu, or they must be written in spoken style.

Neither method is as difficult as you might think. Whether you are chatting privately to a prospect, or publicly to a gathering; on radio or TV; to colleagues or staff; to press or public – the essence of success lies in two words: *chat* and *relax*. Watch successful presenters in any medium and you will see that they chat and relax with you.

Naturally, the style of relaxed presentation will differ but you must still talk *to* people and not *at* them, and try to get their minds *with* and not *against* you.

How, then, can you prefabricate words, set them out on paper, and then read them, so that they sound relaxed? My method is swift and practical – I 'write' almost nothing (except when I 'top and tail' my mail). Every word in every article or book, including all those in this one, goes onto tape. My most precious working possessions are three tiny dictating machines. Why three? Because I give them such a pounding that one is usually under repair; and if the second may go wrong with no third one available, I feel insecure.

The other essential is plenty of tapes. They are cheap enough for you to keep a supply in your briefcase, your car, your home and your office. When you travel abroad, take plenty – you never know when you will need them.

You can talk to your machine as though you are talking to your audience. If you write for a newspaper, you cannot imagine the readers, so you chat to the editor or to the person who has commissioned your work or who will decide whether or not it should be published. If you are preparing a pitch, address your audience.

With enough practice, you should forget the machine altogether. Even if, like myself, you dictate all the punctuation, you will soon find that the knack becomes so natural and the machine goes almost unnoticed.

Once your piece is typed, read it out – aloud, if it is later to be spoken. If it has already emerged once from your mouth, it is far more likely to be well-spoken a second time than any handwritten epic. Even if you have to make massive corrections, or redictate all or part of your effort, the time taken will still be far less than with the same words written by hand.

If you are used to operating a word processor, so that words flow out of your mind into your fingers and out onto the keyboard, then you should try the technique of that master letter writer, Alistair Cooke. He speaks his words over the top of his typewriter at the same time as his fingers type them.

If you are preparing an oral presentation, speak your words first and then, one way or another, get the essentials onto cards or, if necessary, onto paper. The fact that most business people and other amateur presenters do the opposite explains why so many of their presentations go awry.

If your secretary types your dictated speech or other presentation onto a word processor, then he or she will be able to correct it easily. So if you omit an idea, or forget a sentence or paragraph, dictate it at the end and it can be slotted into its proper place.

11

The Four Questions

Preparing to win the pitch means answering The Four Questions we briefly referred to in Chapter 2. These are:

WHO? Who are your prospective customers or clients, your quarry, your audience? What company, firm, organization division or set-up? Also, what sort of environment will they provide, where will you present and in what sort of atmosphere?

WHAT? What do they want? To win, you must be market-led. You must be careful to ask and to answer this question before you move on to the next. Listen before you speak. Only when you have targeted your audience and their requirements do you move to the next question.

WHY? Why are you investing your resources? What is your message? Who are your audience and what do they require; what are you most likely to sell to them?

HOW? How should you put your case? What documentation or visual aids should you use, and when and how?

12

Who?

Step one to success in any relative pitch must be to *target your audience*; to recognize who you are aiming at; to spot your quarry, and then to get and to hold them firmly in your sights.

Do not start preparing your pitch until you know who will be judging it. You cannot select your theme or your team until you have at least a general idea of the nature of your prospective clients or customers.

So you start with *research*. Deploy your forces to find out everything they can about the company or firm that will receive you – in particular, about the section or group within that organization which you hope to serve.

The more you know about those who judge you the better your chances. Not only will your aim be better, but the fact that you have taken pains will indicate that you are painstaking!

Next, try to discover which individuals will be making the assessment. 'Who?' means not only a company or an organization but also the people. If you can *personalize* the pitch that will help to reduce your tension.

Finally, try to find out who will actually make the decision.

According to a cabinet colleague former Chancellor of the Exchequer, Nigel Lawson, attended a Conservative party lunch, where the waiter handed round a basketful of rolls, served with an elegant pair of tongs. He placed a roll and a wrapped piece of butter on each person's plate. Not unreasonably, the Chancellor asked the waiter for a second pat of butter.

'I'm very sorry, sir,' the waiter replied. 'It's one butter for each dinner.'

'I don't think you know who I am,' said the eminent guest. 'I'm Nigel Lawson. I'm Chancellor of the Exchequer. I am the author of the economic miracle. I sit at the right hand of Mrs Thatcher. Please can I have another pat of butter?'

'I don't think you know who I am, Mr Lawson,' said the waiter.

'No, I don't,' said Mr Lawson, 'Who are you?'

The waiter paused and drew himself up to his full height: 'I am the waiter in charge of the butter!'

When it comes to pitches, what matters is to spot the person in charge of the butter. He or she may chair the session, but not always. Lord Prior is Chairman of GEC, but few doubt that Lord Weinstock takes the decisions.

At a less imperial level of power, many decision-takers prefer to let others do the chairing. To take an example in our own sphere, the head of the company, firm or division may chair the pitch, but the training director or manager will pick the winner.

13

Where?

When you stage a performance, you organize the stage: which is fine when you control your own environment, but which seldom works when you are pitching. Your quarry decides not only who wins, but also the place, type and (usually) the layout of the battleground.

You and your opponents will probably be received in a boardroom. Your hosts will be ranged on one side of the table, you and your team on the other. You will march in through the door to be greeted by those who will decide. After a ritual handshake, they will signal you to your seats. They will then invite you to make your presentation.

So how much flexibility does this allow you? At worst, you can fix your own line-up, putting the person chairing in the centre, the next two in importance on either side of him or her, and any others to the sides. At best, you can discuss the venue in advance: to know how you will be received and placed will help you to acclimatize yourself.

If you are using visual aids, the layout and preparation becomes doubly important. For instance, if you will need overhead projection, who will provide the projector and the screen and how can they be best used? If you use 35 mm, perhaps they can hold the session in a room with back projection facilities?

In those (comparatively rare) cases where a major pitch is held in a large hall, will you need amplification? If so, then check that it is both available and efficient.

One classic rule in communication is to *remove barriers*. Do not attempt to talk across a desk or a table. Draw up comfortable chairs and leave the space between you clear of obstructions.

Addressing an audience from a platform? At least consider moving around the table to the front. Or put your notes onto the lectern, but stand at its side. The removal of the object between you and your listeners has both symbolic and atmospheric effect.

Unfortunately, when you pitch, the barrier will probably be

immovable. You may sit around or across a table, but the table will be there. And that makes the task both of interviewers and contestants more difficult. It is easier to judge when both sides are relaxed, some hosts start or finish a pitch over the standing drink – though not, alas, enough. If you are faced with drinks before you pitch, be careful – drunken pitching is dangerous!

14

What Do They Want?

You will know what *you* want to sell: that's not the point. What matters is what *they* will be prepared to buy.

Franklin D. Roosevelt always reckoned that people never listened to what was said to them and would praise a President's casual words as a matter of course. So, for his own amusement, he would sometimes greet guests with the words: 'So good to see you. I murdered my grandmother this morning!' The guests would invariably respond with polite approval. Only once did the President come upon an attentive listener. She nodded at his outrageous remark, then replied with grave diplomacy: 'Mr President, I'm sure she had it coming to her!'

When you have answered the question of 'Who?' you have only started on the road to 'What?'. When you can assess your prospectives you can make a shrewd guess at their perspectives. But that is not enough. So how do you find the answer to the question?

As a start, read and re-read whatever documents your quarry have sent you. These may be totally useless for your purpose: a note or a letter, perhaps, confirming the time and place and possibly (although not certainly) saying how pleased they will be to see you. You may, however, get a more specific tender document (by whatever name) setting out what your hosts require.

Once you know what is wanted, your task is to satisfy those hosts that you will provide it. You may be able to improve on their requirements, to suggest useful variations or additions, or even cost-effective reductions. But it is arrogant stupidity not to offer what the market seeks. Product-led pitches seldom succeed.

15

Your Message – Why?

The purpose of a pitch should be clear from beginning to end. The start sets the tone; the finish decides whether the message is remembered. Far too many pitches simply fade into anti-climax. As the last sentence droops to its end, speakers say 'thank you' and collapse gratefully back into their seats.

Your conclusion and your message should emerge from your final sentence – with your voice and your audience uplifted. Not to give the message at the end of your pitch is like going fishing and casting an unbaited hook into the water.

So work out your message in advance; spell it out from your early words; and leave it well sunk into your audience as you depart. Nothing so becomes a good pitch as an excellent conclusion. Nothing so destroys it as a sentence without end, an end without message. End *up* – with a climax, not with a limp 'thank you'. Pause. Lift up your voice and your audience will leave uplifted.

Of course, if you don't know your message, then you cannot expect to put it across. 'Surely', you say, 'one would not be so idiotic as to go pitching without knowing one's own products?'

Don't you believe it. Consider how often you have been pitched into battle without having had time to put your case together. That includes not only doing your research into the first two questions but also sorting out your third.

16

What's the Point?

In every beauty contest, there's one winner who wins on one point. That point may be anything from special understanding of the client's business or territory, to getting the financial terms exactly right, from appreciating the Chairperson's passion for (say) a particular type of architecture, to the treasurer's dislike for a special kind of funding.

As a young barrister, I was called into the office of my distinguished friend and head of chambers, Charles Lawson. He was almost hidden behind vast bundles of papers, tied up with red tape.

'When's that case on?' I asked him.

'Tomorrow, my boy,' he said. 'And I've just got the papers.'

'Well, you've had it haven't you? You'll never get through that lot,' I said.

'Of course I will. There's only one point in any case. And in this one, I've found it! One point and all the rest is illustration!'

'How did you find it, Charles?'

'Experience. You sniff it out. And I know who's hearing the case. You must know your judges.'

That's it: you learn through experience and if you haven't got that experience, get a colleague onto the job. If neither of you can do it, buy in the experience you need. You need a sharp nose, to sniff out the point, and a sharp mind, to suss out the judges.

This may be about the shortest chapter in the book, but it's the most important.

Part 2

PRESENTATIONAL SKILLS

Be Yourself

Why is it that people who are charming, friendly and articulate in private conversation become wooden, charmless, remote, tongue-tied and wordless the moment they go public? Why, if the presentation is formal, does their backbone wobble and their knees knock, even if they stay seated?

The symptoms of this personality change are almost invariable:

- Speakers avoid eye contact. They look at the floor or ceiling, or anywhere other than at their audience. They swivel their eyes, looking shifty and dishonest.
- They sit forward, elbows on table, hunched and hostile and as visibly screwed up physically as they are churned up mentally.
- If they stand, their fingers twist, their hands gyrate and their bodies jerk, with their heads sunk forward and their eyes downcast.
- Above all, instead of speaking ordinary, relaxed English, they adopt an unreal persona – not their own, but that which they believe others would expect them to adopt when making a formal presentation. They become pompous and formal.
- They speak too quickly, gabbling and rushing towards the end.

Do you sit back in the chair, relaxed and obviously at ease when at home? Then do not lean forward when you talk to your colleagues, your board, your customers or clients, actual or potential. You will not only show relaxed authority if you sit back but also retain the flexibility of occasional forward movement.

Colleagues and I teach and train all levels of business people, plus professionals at every level up to the very top. Our single most important, and often most difficult, task is to induce people to be themselves.

If you are talking to one person, eyeball to eyeball, your eyes should maintain contact. 'All the time he was talking to me, he was looking over my shoulder,' is, however, a common complaint.

So do not lose eye contact with your audience just because the moment or the occasion is formal.

18

Appearance – Dress and Body Language

Former Soviet dissident Anatoli (Natan) Sharansky appeared at an extremely posh dinner in the ballroom of London's Grosvenor House Hotel. He wore a lounge suit with a white, open necked shirt (everyone else was in dinner jacket). A tiny, bald man, he had none of the appearance of a hero. 'You must not take yourself too seriously,' Sharansky told us. 'People expect you to comply with convention. In my case, that means that I am not allowed to wear a tie. And today, I am dying to wear a tie!'

For most of us, pitching is a serious and conventional business: you are meant to 'look the part' – which means, dressing for it. Exceptions can be made for architects, advertising people or pop artists, who are allowed extravagance in their dress. For the rest of us, however, we must look the part. Unfortunately, that means traditional dress.

You want to be authoritative, distinguished, sound and sensible? Then wear a dark suit, with a modest tie. Start assessing your appearance from the top of your head and work down. Do you groom your crowning glory or allow it to dominate you? Does your shirt collar wrinkle or appear over your jacket? Does your tie lie straight? Is your jacket well-cut? Are your trousers the right length?

Remember the importance of body language. You may usefully study Dale Carnegie's classic *How to Make Friends and Influence People*, and Desmond Morris's *The Naked Ape* and *Manwatching* should give your presentations an extra dimension of excellence.

Eye contact is crucial to successful speechmaking, whether you are seated or on your feet. Lowering or swivelling your eyes, or failing to 'look people straight' in theirs are classic symptoms of nervousness. The more your stomach wobbles, the more you should hunt for a friendly face in your audience and talk to it, eyeball to eyeball.

Don't be rigid. Emphasize through an upheld finger; count with several.

There are several things you can safely do with your hands when you stand. Hold the lectern or rostrum before you, grip the edge of the table, put them behind your back, à la Duke of Edinburgh. Or simply hold the cards for your notes, firmly and calmly in front of you. Better still, rest them on the top of a chair back.

Keep your gestures to a minimum. They should emphasize your words, not detract from their meaning. A contemptuous shrug, an occasional accusing finger, a reference to the heavens and hand point to the sky – all have their place in the skilled speaker's repertoire.

If you wear spectacles try using them as an occasional weapon. To emphasize a point, remove them gently from your nose, hold them still in your hand, bend forward and glare at your audience, brandish your glasses and then return them to your nose and your speech to its theme. Even the odd jab with the closed spectacles can be dramatic and useful.

If you are sitting to deliver your presentation, sit upright, with your bottom tucked into the angle between the seat and the back of the chair. Relax, with your shoulders back. If your chair has arms, rest yours on them. Otherwise, put them into your lap or even gently and still on the edge of the table.

Your facial expression should match your topic. President Jimmy Carter used to speak with a fixed grin on his face. Eventually, a professional teacher of presentation showed him on a video screen how wicked it looked to preserve that smile when talking about, for instance, those who had died in Vietnam. He stopped.

Whether you sit or stand will depend, of course, on the number of people and the environment, and what will feel right in the circumstances of your pitch. Given the choice, though, stand. Standing allows you to dominate easily and automatically. Your voice projects better and your eye contact should be easier.

19

Voice Production

The human chest is a sound box. The voice should reverberate and carry. As a stringed instrument gains its volume through the resonance of its sound chamber, so the human voice should resonate through the chest.

Try saying the word 'war'. Through your throat and voice alone, it produces a puny sound. Now take a deep breath, put your head on your chest and sigh out the word until you can feel the vibration. Deep and resonant sound reverberates an idea to immense effect.

The opposite also applies. To attract and hold the attention of an audience, you do not need to shout at them. The dramatic effect of a whisper may be intense.

Remember to vary the volume and tone of your speech, but always within the hearing of your listeners. Address the woman in the back row. Imagine she is deaf – she may be.

Take special care not to drop your voice at the end of a sentence. Thoughts should rise to a climax, not fade with the final breath of a phrase. To avoid monotony, vary tone, speed and volume.

Words do not emerge from closed mouths. You may not consider this an especially brilliant observation, but if you saw the number of top people we train in presentation skills who speak like ventriloquists' dummies, you would be amazed. 'Open your mouth, please,' we implore the executive, whose confidential whispers go unheard because he scarcely moves his lips. 'If ever you lose your job, sir, you should apply for another one as a ventriloquist's dummy!' He thinks we're joking.

If you do not open your mouth sufficiently wide, you cannot project your voice through it. For sound, you need breath. Full voice needs open mouth.

Take this book to a mirror. Read out a short sentence. Then repeat it several times, as naturally as you can. Watch. Is your mouth opening? Are your words coming out loud, crisp and clear?

It may be true that the best way to get some people to agree with you is to keep your mouth shut. But if you are forced to speak, then please open it.

20

Nerve Control

If you don't feel nervous at the start of your pitch, the time has come to worry. You need nervous tension to release your adrenalin, to sharpen and tone up the functions of body and mind. Treat your anxiety with expectant understanding. It will be your ally.

Accepting, then, that pre-presentation nerves are an inevitable necessity, how can you control them?

First, recognize that once you start moving, they will disappear on their own. Runners may retch as they limber up, but never once they are in their starting blocks. Professional public speakers may shake before they begin, but once their first words ring out they stop worrying that their vocal chords will freeze.

Second, remember that your feelings are internal and your audience will not know of them unless you are inexperienced enough to tell them. Therefore, do *not* say 'I am a bag of nerves' or any equivalent. Instead, do:

- sit back, or stand upright.
- pause before you start talking.
- make and keep eye contact with your listeners.
- take a deep breath before you start. Hold it. Then release it slowly.

Avoid whatever form of nervous twitch is your personal affliction. Do not:

- put your hand in front of your mouth – you will muffle your words while leaving your frayed nerve endings visible.
- keep your hands in your pockets – a slovenly discourtesy made worse if you rattle coins or keys.
- fiddle with a pen, jiggle your handbag, tap your fingers or rub your hands together.
- twist your hair, excavate your ear, pick at your nose (however

delicately), open and close buttons of your jacket, or engage in any other of those less entrancing pursuits of the nerve-ridden.

Above all, come to your presentation prepared with adequate notes, simply laid out; knowing your case, and confident that you can deal with your subject. Your nerves can then return to their quietude and you can make your presentation at your ease. That said, here are a few hints to help you either to control your nerves or at least not to show how you feel:

- Take whatever position, sitting or standing, that suits you best. Sometimes, you have no choice, but often you can ask, 'Do you mind if I sit?' or 'If you have no objection, I shall talk to you standing.'
- Do not be afraid to change your position during the course of your presentation. Sit back, with your rear end tucked into the angle of the chair, but do not be afraid to lean forward to emphasize a point. If standing, put one foot ahead of the other and stay still. But if you then want to move around, do so – deliberately.
- If you are superstitious, by all means keep your favourite mascot or charm in your pocket or handbag, but do not rely on it so much that if one day you forget it, your confidence collapses.
- If *one* pre-presentation drink will really relax you, or a tranquillizer stop you from coughing or retching, then take one. But test your reactions first on some other, unimportant day, in case you end up befuddled. If possible, avoid both drink and drugs: they dull reactions.

Not long ago, that most apparently confident of people, Prime Minister Thatcher, was asked whether she was nervous in the House of Commons. She replied: 'I am nervous every time I go to the House of Commons. Every time I go in, I think "Now look love, keep calm. Concentrate!" So as I get up, yes, I'm desperately nervous.

'Believe you me, if I go to Wimbledon or to the Cup Final, I know exactly how those people feel when they walk out on to the pitch or onto the court – nervous, frightened to death until the game starts and then they lose themselves in the game. And that's the only way to do it.'

21

Stress

Every beauty contest means stress. Stress kills. But statistics show that the most vulnerable people are not those either at the top or at the bottom – they are those immediately below the top, striving for success but not quite making it.

Stress, of itself, is inevitable and, if properly harnessed, useful: it sets the adrenalin aflow. If we do not get excitement from our work, we are bored. Horror films and funfair rides are artificial substitutes for that real and joyful thrill which working hours should provide but so seldom do.

Beauty contests are a form of lottery. So why do normal, healthy people take part in this or any form of gambling? Necessity, yes – but also the excitement of the chase. The higher the stakes, the less you can afford to lose, the greater the pressure. Ask successful businesspeople why they keep on with their work long after they have all the money they need for the rest of their healthy days. It's at least partly for the fun of it, for the self-induced stress which is the breath of the entrepreneur's life.

I am often asked how I cope with so many jobs at one time and in one day. Part of the answer is good time management and lively, bright and well-trained partners and assistants. But the major reason is that I don't make the distinction between work and pleasure. What pleasure could be greater than the stressful danger of parliamentary Question Time, when your political opponents are happily waiting for your words to dry up? Or the elation when a presentation, speech or pitch succeeds?

So how do you deal with stress?

Don't bottle it up. The form of release depends on your nature and your constitution. I once watched an uncle exploding with unexplained rage, to his wife and at home. The anger was apparently directed at her, but for no very good reason.

'Never mind,' my aunt said to me. 'He has to keep a rein on

himself all the time at work. If he can't let rip at me, he'll have a heart attack. If he does, I may have one – that's my contribution to the business!' (Both uncle and aunt lived to be old and neither died from a bad heart.)

So if you can release your stress by pounding the pavement, bashing a punchbag or smashing a squash ball, then fine. Otherwise, it is better to bellow than to bust.

Control your stress by taking a series of slow, deep breaths. Recognize what is happening to you as the pressure comes. Control it with your mind.

An honest businessman was charged with setting light to his own warehouse. He climbed into the witness box heavily tranquillized and totally incapable of answering questions. He was convicted and sentenced to three years in jail. It took a 12-month campaign to get his case back to the Court of Appeal, to prove that he could not have been guilty. Drugs were his downfall.

The same applies to drink. As with driving, so with pitching: alcohol may make you feel better, but it will dull your mind.

Instead, prepare. Know your subject so that when you hear your voice, the stress will drop away. Above all, *concentrate*.

22

Stand and Deliver

'Give me a firm place to stand,' said Archimedes, 'and I will move the earth'. He might have said, 'Stand firmly and you are set to move your audience'.

As any toddler will tell you, there is an art to standing. Adult orators too soon forget it.

As a start and at the start, rise before you shine. Say not one word until your feet are firmly in place, your clothing and your notes arranged to your satisfaction, your audience held with your eye.

To start before you stand erect has been described as '*oratus interruptus*'. To pause before you start takes confidence and skill, but is an absolute essential if you do not wish your beginning to fall limp.

To stand *with* ease, stand *at* ease, legs apart and one foot slightly in front of the other. Relax the body and you can then concentrate on balance in speech. With your chest upright and forward, you can produce sound with the least effort and to maximum effect.

Watch any accomplished opera singer. (Not the modern marvels with microphones, I mean those who have been taught to produce fine and varied sound with the instruments with which God has endowed them.) You do not need the training or the talent of a great singer if your words are to live. If you want to achieve success through your words and to avoid oratorical death, stand up for your case.

Once your pitch is moving, you may move with it. You are not a tree, rooted to one spot: you may stroll to your flip chart or your overhead, towards or away from your audience, as the spirit or the subject moves you. Remember:

- Never turn your back on your audience, except for the occasional moment when you are actually writing on your flip charts.

- Never talk to your audience unless your eyes are on them.

If you are using amplification, then make sure that your mike is mobile. Plan in advance and, if possible, make your choice between:

- A neck mike, which hangs without effort. Advantage – you can forget it. Disadvantage – you probably will, tripping over the cord and ripping the mike from your neck, which is most undignified. Also, you cannot adjust it.
- A radio mike. Expensive and liable to interference from, for example, radio cabs.
- A roving mike, clipped initially to a stand, but able to be held by hand. Keep your elbow tucked into your side and the mike will remain the same distance from your mouth, no matter what yours may be from your audience.

The longer your talk, the more appropriate it becomes to introduce action, movement and variety. The more complex the subject, the greater the need for well-prepared visual aids. There is no law against at some stage taking a seat. The only vital rules when you move from standing to sitting, or back again, are to take your time; pause; and stay silent while you rise or fall.

At the start of your speech or presentation, then, rise to the occasion – with calm, relaxed authority. At its end, summarize your content, emphasize your message, work up to your climax. End in certainties. Your beginning should be an indication of your end, and you should finish as you began – on your feet until that last moment of vital control.

The Canadian humorist, Stephen Leacock, wrote of Lord Ronald: 'He said nothing; he flung himself from the room, flung himself up on his horse and rode madly off in all directions!' When you stand and think on your feet, you say your piece; fling yourself nowhere; and direct your words and your body in the required direction only.

23

Low Key

As with the words, so with the voice – low key is usually best. The higher the voice, the lesser the impact, or, as an opera fan once said, 'If anything is too silly to say, you can always sing it.'

Most people enjoy the music of their own voices. Good communicators turn down the volume and adjust the tone. The greater the call for sincerity and trust, the more subtle the sound should be.

In great, past generations of legal advocates – the era of Clarence Darrow in the United States and F. E. Smith (Lord Birkenhead) in Britain, for example – the florid oration, and especially the melodramatic address to the jury, were standard fare. Today is the time of the more gentle and sincere approach, the cajoling of the mind.

An American politician was once asked how you could tell when President Richard Nixon was telling the truth. 'When he clenches his fists and shakes them,' he replied, 'you know that the President is telling the truth. When he holds up his hands to the skies and twists his chin as he speaks, you know that he is telling the truth. But when he opens his mouth . . .'

Brevity and the soft word are the sisters of trust and sincerity. Successful pitching requires both.

24

Time and Brevity

'I'm sorry that I had to write such a long letter,' said Britain's first Prime Minister, Robert Walpole, 'but I did not have time to write a short one.'

When Churchill was asked how long he took to prepare a speech, he answered 'If it's a two-hour speech, ten minutes is enough. But if it's a ten-minute speech, I'll need two hours.'

Work at being brief and concise and your message will stand out clearly and simply. Few audiences have the patience to sort out your message from a cloud of fluff and filler. If you ramble on; if you do not compact your thoughts, your pitch and your message; if you overrun your time – you've got problems. So study the art of brevity.

Begin by thinking about the overall length of your pitch, bearing in mind that it will almost always take longer to deliver than you expect. Add at least 20 percent to rehearsal time.

When solicitors instruct counsel to advise, to draft a document, or to appear in court, they send briefs. A brief is a summary of the facts, with comments. A first-class brief condenses the facts, lists and draws attention to the main features of essential documents, indicates the solicitor's own views, and specifies what the barrister is asked to do – all in a few pages.

Keep sentences short, comprehensible, and clear. If you go on too long, your listener or reader will forget the beginning before you reach the end. Keep your words short too. You do not need pompous and ponderous language to impress.

During two presentational skills sessions – one with top executives, the other with professionals – I jotted down some of the long words used by delegates. You will find them at the end of this chapter – along with their brief brothers. Each time you are bored at (say) a conference, add to the list yourself. Collecting other people's errors is not only a useful way of passing time, it is a way of learning how to avoid such errors yourself.

If you are suffering from a lifetime addiction to jargon then you cannot expect to change overnight – but you must start trying now.

The process can, of course, be taken too far. I once commissioned a distinguished academic to write a 'short history' of an organization. He did just that: it was very short indeed.

The book was launched at a ceremony, chaired by the President of that organization, who spoke for about three minutes. Ivan Lawrence QC MP expressed our thanks to the author, as follows: 'Mr President, I greatly enjoyed your speech. It gave me the time to read the book!'

Now for the long or pompous words on my list and their suggested replacements:

Attempt or Endeavour	=	Try
Perceive	=	See
Beware of	=	No
In this moment of time/In this day and age/Currently/Presently	=	Now
Acquire or purchase	=	Buy
Dispose of	=	Sell
Bring to a conclusion/Conclude	=	End
Demonstrate	=	Show
However	=	But
Consequently/Therefore/Accordingly	=	So
Indicate	=	Show
Envisage	=	Expect, or see
Request	–	Ask
In what manner	=	How
Manner	=	Way
Subsequently	=	Then, or afterwards
Proceed	=	Go
Adjacent to	=	Next to, or near
Approximately	=	About
Commence	=	Start
Assist	=	Help
It was necessary for us to	=	We had to, we needed to
Obtain	=	Get
Opportunity	=	Chance
Assistance	=	Help

You are able to	=	You can
Arrested	=	Stopped
This permitted us to	=	We could
The remainder	=	The rest
In order to	=	So as to

Finally, take time to repeat. If you have made a list, then you must repeat it. The same goes for important points made in a sequence that you want your audience to remember. For example, 'So let me sum up. We are immensely enthusiastic about your project. The three reasons that I have given are . . . , . . . and . . . . We know that we can provide the swift, effective and reactive service that you rightly require.'

25

Time to Pause

For how long would you say that the average person can concentrate? Surprisingly, not more than about 1.5 to 2 minutes.

So how do you hold people's attention for longer periods? You change your pace or style. You add a touch of wit or humour. You tell a story or anecdote. Or you simply . . . pause.

Taking your time is one of the most crucial oratorical skills. Breathing time for yourself means thinking time for your audience: omit either and you reveal your lack of confidence.

At the start of your presentation, wait until you have the full, undivided and silent attention of your audience. Whether you are speaking to three, to 30 or to 300 people, the principle is precisely the same. For your audience to pay attention to you, you must *demand* that attention from the start, nor must you start until you have that attention, or you cannot hope to hold it.

Unless the Chair demands silence for you, stand – or, if necessary, sit – erect. Look your audience in the eye, and command silence with body language. Wait for silence and attention and under no circumstances move into your presentation until you get it. Begin with 'Ladies and gentlemen' or 'Mary Sharp' or simply 'Good morning'.

The pause is the toughest test of confidence for any speaker. You must wait until your audience is silent before you begin. Pause before key words and phrases, and especially as you build up to your climax. Recognize that you need time for yourself and for your audience, to take breath and to think.

We all recognize the human fountain gushing in a ceaseless flow on to an audience soon drenched in the spray of ideas. That was my style, when I began my apprenticeship in that debating society which is one of the toughest orator training grounds, the Cambridge Union. It took three weeks of lessons, two hours a weekday, with a remarkable teacher, to learn to throw my voice, my ideas and my message, with a variety of speed, mood and tone.

My tutor was skilled and bright. So why did it take him three weeks when we can usually achieve much the same results in two days? The answer lies in the magic of audio-visual equipment. Listen to yourself, breathless, monotonous, unremitting. Watch yourself, as your eyes retreat to your notes, your speech incessant through fear of silence. Sound and pictures combine to teach more than any trainer.

Our clients take their video cassettes home. They can then play them, to the delight and laughter of their families. They can watch their own improvement as the sessions proceed.

Harold Macmillan once said, 'The most important technique for any orator . . . if you can do it . . . is . . . the pause. . . .' Practise it. And do it.

26

Audience Involvement

You must keep your audience involved and interested. The team is there to talk, but always look for ways to listen.

The key word in the pitcher's language is 'you'. Conversely the pronoun 'I' with economy. 'We' can, however, be useful. When you are presenting as a team, it serves to suggest that your views should be shared by your colleagues, the company, public opinion, the industry, the nation.

One way of involving your audience is to ask questions. Do not begin with, 'We'll take your questions at the end'; but weave them into your pitch, adding variety without effort.

Always try to personalize your pitch. Being impersonal is only appropriate in the rare cases in which you are selling detachment. Even then, relate to your audience by using their individual names. You must judge on each occasion whether first or surnames are appropriate. If you are pitching to retain existing clients, it would usually (though not always) be wrong to use surnames.

Involve the senior, most distinguished and powerful listeners. For example: 'Mr Green, you are Marketing Director and responsible for this territory. Would you care to comment on this approach or perhaps add to it?'

If the audience appears restless, change your speed, your pitch and your approach. Bring in someone else from your team; ask questions; look from person to person; use interruptions to flavour your talk. A passing aircraft, the invading tea trolley, a distant explosion – refer to them and show that you are alert. Be ready to use unfriendly interruptions as a tool. As every skilled political speaker knows, hecklers bring an audience to life, to its feet, onto your side.

Remember with kindness those who may wish to ask questions but are afraid of appearing foolish – perhaps through not understanding jargon with which they feel they should be familiar.

Always take the blame yourself: for example, 'That's a good question. I don't think I have explained that part thoroughly enough. It works like this. . . .'

You will also need to develop ways of *controlling* your audience; of directing the argument, controversy or discussion towards and along the themes that you have in mind. This requires total concentration. You must be constantly alert; you must listen to what your listeners are saying and to how they are saying it. You must feel how the meeting is 'moving' and, if you do not like the direction, shift it.

One way of doing this is to bring in someone who you know will put the viewpoint you need – either because it happens to be yours or as a balance to the discussion.

27

Boredom

Boring and being bored both have curious effects on those who hold or take part in beauty contests. If you find your own case so unexciting, how can you expect to infuse your audience with its impact? So the usual rule is: bore your audience and you kill your presentation.

As a young barrister, I was once 'led' by a distinguished and usually witty Queen's Counsel in a lengthy fraud trial at the Old Bailey. Instead of his usual animated style, he preferred to drone tediously on. 'Why?' I asked him.

'Because if we're lucky,' he replied, 'the jury will get as bored with the charges as you are. And as they will probably not understand the case, there is a chance that our unworthy clients may be acquitted!' They were.

A man who did the same for the Commons was my late friend and then Attorney General, Sam Silkin. Never known for his sparkle in public, he was brilliant at emptying the Chamber when coping with some real error by his Cabinet or himself. He would put down his head, lose all eye level contact with his audience and read out his brief with dire monotony. 'Bor-ing!' the House would cry out; Members would either drop off or drop out. The holes in his case were hidden by the misery of enduring his deliberate sermons.

Still, it is no fun to create the illusion of eternity. The art of boring to death should be used rarely. In its place it may work miracles, but usually it spells disaster.

So what should you do? You are not, after all, a comedy act. But when you present your case, you are *on stage, you are part of the entertainment business*. The word 'entertainment' comes from the French 'entre' and 'tenir': you create a bond between your ideas and your mind and those of your audience. Fail to hold or grip your audience and you will lose.

You can enliven your presentation by remembering the three Es

– Enthusiasm, Energy and Excitement. Salt your words with humour, spice them with wit, pepper them with an occasional anecdote, story or illusion. Keep yourself and your audience awake.

28

Humour

Wit and humour are essential to pitches – provided that they are appropriate to the occasion, to the audience and to the presenter. Comedian Bob Monkhouse offers the following four rules on humour:

1 Whether it is a joke, a story, a one liner or an anecdote – *you* must think it funny. If it does not tickle your sense of humour, don't use it.

2 The humour must *suit* you – your style, your personality, your approach. For instance; you may be confident with stories but find dialect difficult: avoid such stories.

3 Humour must suit the audience. It is not enough that it is funny to you and suits your style. If it does not fit your audience, it may do harm.

4 Do not offend. Avoid the risqué, rude, vulgar and obscene. Pitching is not a stag dinner.

Be especially careful with dialect stories. Satire is dangerous, unless you belong to the group satirized. I have a splendid repertoire of Jewish stories which I enjoy telling. But I rarely appreciate tales about Jews told by non-Jews. I also leave jokes about blacks to friends who are black, about Catholics to friends who are Catholic, etc. (Unless you happen to be one, in which case help yourself, but still watch out for the personal.)

Personal jokes are rarely acceptable. Most people are touchy about their own names: 'Ah yes, I can remember your name easily, it's like grovel, isn't it?' is not the best way to win my affection.

Most people enjoy making jokes about their own profession – so let them get on with it.

If a witticism or a gag falls flat, never mind. Pretend that it was not intended to be funny and carry on with the serious business of selling.

Timing is particularly important when using humour. The joke, witticism or humorous thrust must be well placed in relation to the presentation and to the mood of the audience, and it must be told at the right pace, with the correct emphasis, and with the appropriate pauses. Listen to any first-class wit at work: at least half the effect is achieved by timing. Listen and imitate.

Don't worry if you cannot think of a suitable story for the occasion – inspiration may arrive as you talk.

Finally, if you have done your homework and can introduce an 'in-joke' or an insider twist, a topical reference or an up-to-date jibe, you will win points. You will be showing understanding and confidence which your opponents are unlikely to be able to match.

All that said, you must, of course, avoid the role of the clown: overdo the spice and you ruin the meal.

29

Names

Two athletes met in the centre of the Olympic Stadium. One said to the other: 'Are you a pole vaulter?' The other replied, 'No. I'm German. But how did you know my name?'

For most people, names are no joke – either because they cannot remember other people's or because they object to others forgetting or mispronouncing their own.

Not long ago, we were successful in a pitch to teach presentational skills to a prominent city firm of surveyors. As always we tried to find out why we had won.

'Your main competitors made it easy for you. Our MD, who was sitting to one side, said to them "Fine. Then tell me who I am and what I do?" Your opponent was completely flummoxed. He did not know.'

In the words of the Bible, 'Know before whom you stand.' (Or sit.) By all means know them by name if you can. As part of your preparation for the contest try to find out who will be judging it. Maybe they produce a brochure with photographs . Remember our first question. 'Who?'

When you are introduced, listen to the names and repeat them – to yourself or to them. Write the names down in front of you, on a plan of the opposite side of the table, each in his or her place – preferably with job titles.

Listen carefully to the pronunciation of names. People can be touchy if others mispronounce.

So how do you remember names? The best method comes from mind expert and President of the Magic Circle, David Berglas. First, repeat the name as often as possible: 'Yes, Mrs Green', 'I agree with you Mrs Green', 'But, Mrs Green, have you considered'.

Then create a word association which reminds you of that name. It should be as weird as possible, for instance, a woman delegate on one of our day courses was Mary Bisky – 'Whisky' a colleague said to me. 'Whisky. Every time you see her, you picture a large bottle of whisky in her hand.' It worked.

A final tip. If you are introducing your own team, you will make a terrible impression, if, under the stress of the moment, you forget their names (which, I assure you, often happens). To avoid that horror, I use another magicians' method. I write the names down on a tiny piece of paper, which I palm (hold invisible in the palm of my left hand). If I forget the names, I know that I can glance down and be reminded. The knowledge that the names are there if I want them shakes me free from panic: I have never yet had to use them.

30

Notes, Quotes and Statistics

Notes are essential reminders for all presenters. Even if you do not use them, the knowledge that notes are to hand – or in hand – gives crucial confidence.

They should, however, be kept to a minimum – the first sentence; the last sentence; and the skeleton. They should contain the flow of ideas; the thread of the speech; reminders of themes; and brief headings for the eye, to direct the flow of speech but not to interrupt it.

Except where you must indulge in quotations, the shorter and clearer the notes, the better. Divide your notes, using block capitals for headings, and underlining in different colours. Set the notes into columns, and lay them out so as to catch your eye, just as you seek to lay out your speech to catch the minds and imaginations of your listeners.

Notes are best made on cards, preferably not larger than normal postcard size. Each theme, paragraph, or arrangements of ideas can then be put onto a separate card. Use one side only; when the ground on a card has been covered, turn it over.

If you run out of time, you can simply skip two or three of the less essential cards, or just summarize them in sentences, and turn them over at speed. They provide your guide without restricting you to an itinerary. They leave you room to manoeuvre and encourage you to think on your feet.

In case you drop your notes, number each card clearly, at the top right-hand corner.

Notes should be guides and pointers, not crutches or stretchers. Holding adequate, brief, memory-jogging notes will give you confidence, but do not look down at them for words, ideas or concepts that you really should know. Indeed, never talk while looking down at your notes. Pause, look at your card or page, then look up and carry on.

Flexibility is vital: be prepared to re-order your notes and shuffle your ideas up to the moment when you rise to your feet – and even as your themes unfold. This is only possible where notes are on cards, with one idea, theme or argument on each. It is impossible where a speech is written out.

Prospective clients or customers will always look at your existing client list, and at the quoted recommendations that your satisfied customers have given you. Your documentation should give prominence to the words of your contented clientele.

Quoting is an art. You may pepper your pitch with apt quotations from others, but keep them short – to quote at length from memory is a form of showing off that is seldom appreciated. You are not engaged in stage soliloquy: to read someone else's words at length is rarely a good alternative to putting thoughts and ideas into your own words. The reading of other people's speeches – or even lengthy parts of them – is usually an error.

Quotations are only worth using if they are thoroughly apt. If your audience is flagging, it is sometimes helpful to 'drag in a joke by its ears'. This legitimate gambit may reduce strain, but the story must be apposite. It is a mistake to thrust an inappropriate quotation into your speech, merely because you have a fond feeling for it.

Attribute the quotation to its true author, if you can. If in doubt, you could try: 'Was it George Bernard Shaw who said . . . ?' Or, 'I think it was Oscar Wilde who once remarked that. . . .' Or if the attribution is to someone in your lifetime, you can seldom go wrong with: 'I once heard President Ford remark on television that. . . .' or 'Did you read the saying, attributed to Mr Kruschev, that. . . .' Who is to prove you wrong?

Make sure that your speech really is *strengthened* by putting the statement concerned in quotation marks – and as coming from a particular author. When trying to convince a British audience to adopt an American practice, it is sometimes better to adopt the trans-Atlantic arguments without stating their origin.

The best quotations come, of course, from the careless mouths of your opponents: 'Today, Mr Jones condemns amalgamation. But who was it who said, just two years ago, and I quote: "Our future depends upon achieving amalgamation. We cannot survive as a small independent unit?" None other than my friend, Mr Jones!'

Quotations from yourself should be avoided: 'Did I not say, six months ago, that . . . ?' Or, 'May I repeat what I said at our trade conference last month?' Unless you have previously been accused

of inconsistency, self-quotation is generally pompous and ego-
tistical.

Similar rules apply to statistics. Use them sparingly.

Several graduates applied for a job with a firm of city
accountants. Each was asked, 'What is twice one?' Each replied,
'Two'. The application who eventually got the job replied, 'What
number did you have in mind, sir?'

When you present statistics, at least indicate their origin –
assuming only that you are not ashamed of it.

Do not presume that others are as conversant with figures or
accounts as yourself. I am constantly amazed by businesspeople
who cannot even read a balance sheet. Try to steer your way
between the cardinal sin of talking down to your audience on the
one hand, and conferring undue knowledge on the other. If in
doubt, explain.

Recognizing that some human beings absorb by ear and others by
eye, but most require a combination of both, and accepting also that
your audience is far more likely to be innumerate than illiterate,
supplement your words with paper – graphs and the rest – and,
where appropriate, with visual aids (see Part 3).

31

Reading

A politician once unkindly remarked that there are two classic contradictions in terms – military intelligence and socialist lawyers! I would add a third: a read pitch.

The object of all presenters should be to project themselves – which means outward to their audience, and not downward onto a script. So do chat informally, using notes or visual aids as your guide.

There are occasions, however, when reading is essential:

- Where every word must be precise because of the dangers of misquotation.
- Where the occasion itself is so important that you decide you must work from a script.

If you must read, make sure you maintain maximum eye contact – look up as much as you can and down as rarely as possible. How can you achieve this miracle? Sir Winston Churchill prepared his speeches word for word, but had them written or typed with their beginnings zig-zagged down the page and wide spaces between sentences. His eye would then catch one sentence and tweak his memory of its wording; he would then look up to and at his audience; and when he looked down again, his mind would take his eye forward onto the next zig or zag of wording.

Top politicians and executives often use autocues. Just as the teleprompt system runs words before the eyes of newsreaders and other broadcasters, so the autocue keeps a moving script before the presenter or speechmaker. Words are projected onto plastic screens, visible to the speaker but not the audience. If your occasion is sufficiently important, you can hire an autocue and operator. Practise, though, before you use it, and keep a script handy in case the contraption hiccups.

If you work from paper, use the following checklist:

- Make sure your scripts are cleanly typed (preferably with large script), and always with wide margins and good spacing between lines.
- End a paragraph on the page it began on. Do not allow a paragraph (or, still worse, a sentence) to flow over from one page to the next.
- Use marks to indicate pauses and words or syllables to be emphasized. These marks may be underlining in different colours or coloured highlights. (I dislike highlights because they destroy, however marginally, the clarity of the script, and you should avoid anything that distracts or complicates the eye or the mind – both should spend maximum concentration on the audience.)

Practise reading your speech. Know your subject and your script, and take special care over words which trip your tongue (such as 'February' and 'particularly', for example – or whatever your own 'word enemies' happen to be).

Finally, take care with speechwriters. Those you use should adapt to your style; do not allow them to use words or phrases which remove your personality and substitute it with theirs.

If you must read, do it with style – your own. Learn the techniques of skilled reading, and practise and use them.

Part 3

DOCUMENTATION AND VISUAL AIDS

32

Pitching on Paper

Paper and its style matter. Choose your paper with care. Check:

- *Quality,* including thickness, feel and appearance.
- *Cost* in relation to both purpose and quantity. Do you wish to impress by style and prestige – or will too fine a quality or too smart an appearance indicate an over-expensive product?
- *Use.* If you intend photocopying from a 'master' sheet onto the presentation paper, make sure your photocopier can cope with the weight and colour of paper you are ordering. Most photocopiers can only cope with white paper, and paper which is too heavy or thick will simply jam in the machine.

Choose with care your style of heading and of printing. Select a logo which will be striking, memorable and appropriate. Balance the size and placing of the print. You may need help from a professional designer or commercial artist – or you may get equally good results from a first-class experienced printer, especially one who knows your own style and approach.

Insist that you get proofs, and that they arrive in good time for you to make any necessary changes. (Changes should be kept to a minimum because they involve expense for the printer which – dependent upon the contract and/or goodwill of the printer or designer – may be passed on, in whole or in part, to you.)

Proof-reading requires great care. Amazing mis-spellings can escape a proof-reader's eye – and once you have had, and approved, the proofs, you can no longer blame the printer if the paper has to be scrapped.

Check the following carefully:

- The relationship between the print (including the varying sizes), the logo and the paper.
- The size of specific lines: for example you will not want 'From

the Managing Director' (or as the case may be) printed too large.
- Make sure that the logo is precisely upright – and, if appropriate, in line and squared up with the paper itself and/or other printing on it.

Remember that one colour printing is cheaper than two; simple printing less costly than embossed or other raised type. Repeated formats, or pages using the same design elements, can reduce costs – both on the initial printing and later.

Choose carefully the colour or colours of: a) the paper itself, and b) the print. From the basic black print on white paper, there are almost endless variations. If you find one that suits you and your product particularly well, you may wish to make it into a 'house colour' – immediately identifiable (at least by regular recipients), and conveying the intended impression of your product, your services or yourself.

Unless you are a bulk buyer, the purchase of the paper itself will depend little on quantity – but it is invariably cheaper to *print* in quantity. Typesetting, preparation of machinery, and the general cost benefits of large-scale production all contribute to high costs for small quantities. Before having a large amount printed, however, check whether you may need to change the paper because:

- The individuals whose names appear on it may move;
- Addresses, telephone numbers, fax or telex details may be altered; or
- You may tire, or think better, of the design, logo, etc.

Shop around for quotes. The cost of the paper itself, and of the printing on it, may vary dramatically.

Give yourself time to make your choice, get your quotations, increase your options, vary your requirements and consult your colleagues or experts. Give your designers and printers time to do the job properly so that you do not have to pay a premium for a rush job. A well-written and presented pitch is well worth the quality paper on which it is printed.

33

Style and Grammar

Whether you present your documentation before, during or after your pitch, style matters. So do grammar and punctuation.

Style, of course, cannot be detached from general layout. Pitchers, like athletes, must get their start and their finish just right if their efforts are to produce winners. The contents must be brief and lucid – and nicely paragraphed. But above all, the style of the words must reflect the *intention* of the pitch.

The words of pitchers are the 'dress' of their thoughts. If these words are inept, slovenly, ill-suited to the occasion, their style will destroy their impact. Style should match circumstances.

With documentation, your accent disappears. Your speech may bear the marks of Belgravia or Bohemia, Brooklyn or Bermondsey, but your writing need receive no overtones from your voice. This may be a great asset because, like it or not, the commercial world is largely snob-ridden. On paper, everyone starts at the same level – pens and word processors are classless instruments. The heavily accented words which you speak into your dictating machine emerge classless, sexless and without indication of ethnic or racial origin. At least, they should.

What can be done, then, to repair broken English? I offer three suggestions. First, read well and widely. Study the financial columns in the newspapers and the form of both companies and race horses. Fill in those odd moments in the train, bus, car or taxi by reading something different. Have you dipped into Hersey or Hemingway? Do you still think that David Copperfield was a character in a film? What of Solzhenitsyn or Graham Greene or Amos Oz? To write well you should read avidly – and the greater your failings as a grammarian, the more you should soak your mind in the rich wine of fine literature.

Finally, do not turn up your nose at formal courses aimed at adults. If you would prefer to remain anonymous, then have one custom-made and get yourself a teacher – the money will be well spent. Try correspondence courses: there are plenty about, and while your tutors may have to advertise their services, there is no need for you to advertise that you are making use of them.

The object of documentation is to propound ideas. Whether you are buying or selling, hiring or firing, praising, decrying, apologising, or negotiating matters not. You are engaging in self-expression, on paper, as an essential part of your pitch. Say what you must (or what you wish) with clarity, but your personality needs expression, along with your views.

34

Structure

Documentation, like the pitch itself, needs a structure. Say what you are going to say; say it; then say what you have said.

Start with a clear first sentence, to catch the reader's interest, to sum up what is to come and to make sure that your words will be taken seriously. Let each idea lead logically on to the next. Jot down your points; set them out in logical order; connect them up with the general theme; then end with your summary.

Design the main body of your documentation so that it can be read conveniently and comfortably, as well as swiftly referred to. Dry facts, lists, graphs, accounts, balance sheets, formulae – all these are better in an Appendix.

Use every available method for making the reader's work easier: references, cross-references and footnotes all help. So does a Contents page at the front or an Index at the back. Your referencing must be precise and clear.

Keep your layout well spaced and neat. Insert headlines as marginal notes, if you wish. Develop your own house style.

Recognize the immediate impact of your stationery, word-processing or printing. Check and double-check for slovenly or careless style or spelling. Whenever possible, use the active and not the passive voice: for example, 'We received your tender documents', *not* 'Your tender documents were received by us'.

Grammar is a giveaway. It places the seal of education on the document of authority – or it shows that the writer is uneducated, 'unlettered' or illiterate. (Which may not matter, if the job you seek is purely technical, but it cannot help.) Do not, however, fear the lively phrase. One word may be effective on its own. Often.

Take care with punctuation. A full stop indicates a break in thought. A comma marks a pause. A semicolon is half a colon and is useful to indicate the end of an item in a list. The colon comes between the semicolon and the full stop – it shows a pause in the flow of thought, but not for long. A dash is useful: it indicates a break in the sentence or list, longer than that shown by a series of dots. Dots indicate that the thought has not ended, even though the sentence or paragraph may have done.

Careful punctuation breaks up a paragraph or sentence. The brisker your chosen style, the more use you will make of the dot and the dash.

35

Visual Aids and Accessories

Words are the essence of pitching. Visual aids and accessories are methods designed to aid and assist presenters. They should supplement, but never supplant, your words. An aid emphasizes the vital, and explains the complex. It adds colour variety and style. It must be selected with care and used with skill.

Always remember that human minds differ – some people can absorb ideas from letters and books, others from lectures and oral lessons. Some minds are photographic, others assimilate through action. Some people who are highly literate are totally innumerate – and vice versa.

Slide and tape-slide presentations
Slides can be presented in many different ways – from the simplest single projector and portable screen, to the sophisticated computer-controlled, multi-projector systems often used in fashion or screen shows.

One useful alternative to the single projector and screen is the self-contained, desk-top machine. The latter projects the slides internally onto a small screen at the front, which is usually about the size of a TV screen. It is only suitable for a small audience, but does not need any black-out, and it is usually portable as no separate screen is required.

Another possibility is the 'dissolve pair'. The slides are split between two projectors so that the presenter can fade from one to the other and eliminate the blank screen between slides. The two projectors are mounted side by side or one on top of the other and are controlled by a 'dissolve unit'. A simple hand control advances the slides. They allow the operator to record a commentary, and then to pulse the tape to advance the slides at the correct points. With the system set up in this way, you can just start the tape and let it roll, as with a video.

There are machines available that enable you to make the tapes yourself, commonly called 'tape-slide presentations', but for best results with these do get professional help – especially with the sound track.

When using an overhead projector, take care not to project a distorted picture. Make sure that the machine is square to the screen. If screen and machine cannot be on the same level, incline the screen. This should reduce 'keystone' distortion, that is widening of the image towards the top.

Make sure that all machinery is tested and ready for use (films laced up in the projector, videos advanced to the start point, slide trays set at zero) before you begin your presentation.

16 mm films
Around 90 per cent of 16 mm films have what is called an 'optional sound track'. Others have, instead, a magnetic sound track – in which case, ensure that your projector is capable of replaying, as not all film projectors have this facility.

36

Transparencies, View Charts, Slides, Flip Charts and Other Aids

Consider – and refer to – the following points when using visual aids:

- Select the best aids for the particular occasion. 35 mm slides, for example, are splendid for large audiences and for showing pictures.
- Do not use visual aids to replace your verbal message. Charts, etc., should either: a) provide the skeleton for your presentation, so as to attract the eye and direct the mind (and later to revive the memory); or, b) illustrate and explain, through graphs, etc., concepts and/or detail which cannot be explained simply, adequately and/or swiftly in other ways.
- Overhead projector transparencies are cheaper and easier to make than slides and can be drawn on during the presentation. But they should be treated with respect – their contents should be carefully thought out and the transparencies themselves professionally produced. (These sheets of clear plastic, usually mounted in card frames, are also known as slides or overheads.)
- Keep the wording on all visual aids to a sensible minimum. This does not mean putting one simple sentence onto a separate transparency, but avoiding a mass of hard-to-assimilate material which is properly divisible into two or more projections.
- Transparencies, etc., should be concise, compact and uncluttered: use abbreviations and symbols to to summarize and to emphasize. Use artwork sparingly and for *results*, not *effect*.
- Remind your graphics department to make the slides with backgrounds clear and light – not obscure and dark. The darker the background, the poorer the view. Green, blue and black come out well on a white background, as black does on yellow.

But red on green, or green on red, are even worse than white on red, orange on black, or red on yellow. Clarity of overhead vision should never be sacrificed for artificial and artistic impression. For best results, use black on white or white on black.

- Use 'funnies' sparingly. Humour is much better presented orally (if only because you can quickly move on and away from a failed joke). If you must use cartoons, caricatures or illustrative, graphic humour, make sure that it is thoroughly professional.
- Choose your overhead projectors or machinery with care. For instance, I dislike those projectors with fans that change the atmosphere when they come on; often do not go off along with the light; and disturb speaker and audience. Watch out especially for those that blow air out sideways, whisking papers all over the place. Better (in any event with a smaller audience) to use a mirror-type, fanless projector.
- Make sure your visual aids are properly set up before your audience arrives, that is focused and with the first slide, transparency, etc., in position.
- The first slide or transparency should generally provide an overall summary – to which you can (especially with transparencies) return, using further projections to fill in the details.
- To point at a slide, you must use (and have ready) a stick or other pointer. For a transparency, you have three possibilities, which can be used in combination, for variety as required:
    1 Point with a pencil, pen or even a finger on the slide itself, casting the shadow of the pointer onto the screen. Put your pen down on the transparency. Do not hold it, or the slightest jiggle or movement will create a major flicker on the screen.
    2 Use pointer or finger on the screen itself – but beware of casting the shadow of your body onto the screen at the same or any time.
    3 Use a sheet to cover up that part of the transparency that you do not require the audience to see – and then move it. (This method can, however, irritate audiences, who find themselves wondering what is hidden, rather than thinking about what is revealed.)
- Changes of transparency should be slick. Hold the replacement in your right hand; remove the existing transparency with your

left and put the new one in its place, all in one movement; and practise until you can put the replacement into a firm, central position without fiddling.

- Make sure that all the audience can see the machine – if some cannot, then move them or the screen.
- Be deliberate – do not jog, jolt or jiggle an item on the screen.
- Talk to your audience, not to the machine – and even if you are reading out what is on the screen, do not turn your back on your audience or put your face down to the machine. Try never to turn your back on your listeners.
- Minimize your own movement and that of the visual aids. Do not distract from the content.
- Use variety in your visual aids – different types, colours, underlining, etc. Visual aids should stimulate interest and not provide a technical message. Check your pens or crayons in advance, and break up the script by usig different colours. Make sure the lettering is large enough to be seen. Use as few words as possible. For instance, do not say 'replaced by' – simply cross out whatever it is that has been replaced.
- If you draw on transparencies, use water-based pens, which can be rubbed out with a damp cloth – not those that require spirit for removal.
- Watch good teachers using blackboards, and use their techniques with your flip charts. Good teachers will ask their audience questions while they write; never remove their eyes from their class for more than a few seconds; and turn sideways when writing, never turning their backs to their audiences for longer than necessary. A mnemonic may help you to remember this: the three Ts – T-ouch the writing; T-urn to the audience; and only then T-alk.
- If you show slides, try not to keep the room in permanent gloom while you talk. Maybe you can place yourself to one side or under a spotlight, or at least turn the light on when the slides are off. Consider reserving slides for start and/or finish, or for one central episode, and leave the light and emphasis on yourself for the rest of the time.
- To avoid the blank spaces of darkness and silence between slides, you could try a 'dissolve pair' projection system (see page 72). However, these prepared slides have to remain in the same order and there is no way in which you can shuffle them. Inflexibility may be a high price to pay for apparent slickness.

- Beware of over-preparation – the over-professionalism too often produced by specialists, for the use of amateurs (auto-cued, word-perfect script, dramatic music and lighting) may be too slick (as well as costly) and will remove your personal impact, which is what distinguishes you from your competitors.
- To make the best of slides, overhead charts, etc., why not provide copies for your audience? This saves them writing, so that they can concentrate on your presentation. As with all other documentation, consider carefully whether you would wish to supply in advance (not generally recommended, because busy people seldom do their homework, and often forget to bring it with them on the day); at the time of presentation for use during its course; or at the end of the presentation, to take home.

The old-fashioned but worthy flip chart will never go out of fashion. At its simplest, it consists of a stack of newsprint attached to a board. With pens or crayons, you illustrate your words, flipping over or tearing off sheets. You may use and re-use prepared flippable charts. (I sometimes use a helpful variant – a white-faced, steel board with magnetic lines, spots and dots, and coloured, water-based pens that write and erase with ease.) When pointing at a flip chart – or a transparency – use your nearest hand or arm, so as not to have to twist your body and turn your back to the audience. The 3Ts (see above) apply as much to flip charts as to other forms of presentation.

Small, compact, flip-over charts are available and are useful for the small pitch or round-the-table presentation.

If you intend to use this or any other sort of visual aid, remember that it must be well and professionally produced – as excellent as your company or firm, your products or your services.

37

Audio-Visual, Film and Disc

To make a pitch permanent, you may put it into type or print. You should also consider the magic of recording – on audio or videotape, on film or on disc. Each is a highly specialized art.

Audio
The beauty of an audio cassette is that listeners can play it at their convenience – at home, in the office or (even more likely) in the car. Then they can replay any part that particularly attracts, repels or baffles them.

At its simplest, you may make your cassette by talking into your tape recorder and leaving it to anyone of minor technical talent to copy. At best, though, your cassette should be professionally made in a studio, with a script prepared.

For a sales cassette, you may manage with minimal voices and rely on the novelty and interest of the material to attract your market. But do remember that the script-writing and recording of these cassettes require skill. The fact that you are capable of speech no more qualifies you to produce an audio cassette than your ability to press the button of a simple camera will turn you into an expert photographer.

So if you make an audio presentation, get expert help. Find a good (preferably recommended) studio, and match the presenta-tion to the content. The time that the job will take depends on those making the recording, both readers and technicians. Some 'fluffs' are inevitable: the recording engineer will stop you from time to time and make you repeat sentences – if only because, for example, you 'pop' a 'p', so that it sounds like gunfire. If you and other presenters are fluent and relaxed readers, you should be able to make a 60-minute tape in three hours of studio time. If you are afraid or inexperienced or both, you should set aside one day – especially if you want to be in on the editing.

The studio will edit your cassette, sending you proof copies. Check them with care, but amend them with discretion – returning to the studio costs time and money.

Once the cassette is approved, production should be swift and painless. Repeat orders are cheap: as with printing, with taping – the first copy costs more than the next 500.

If you are serious about hooking listeners to your pitching material, look into the costs of cassette presentation. The fact that the UK companies make money from business audio cassettes should not deter you from using them as an appropriate vehicle for your needs.

Finally, if you cannot find the right people to use their own voices, try employing professional speakers. This may save on studio costs and give better end results.

Video

Do not underestimate the importance of video presentation. It can be shown on a very large screen (up to five feet diagonal), and any number of copies can be made relatively cheaply. It can also be used for all sorts of other purposes, including showing on the company stand at an exhibition, staff training and internal presentations – nearly all boardrooms now have video equipment.

The best way to make a video or film presentation is to get someone else to do it for you, so employ experts to make the video and to bring in, and operate, the equipment.

38

Amplification – and Microphone Techniques

You will do most of your pitching around a table and your voice should produce enough sound on its own. Sometimes, though, you may have to put your case to a major gathering, and will need amplification. So how can you make a microphone your ally?

First, adjust it to your height. Whether it is a standing or a table model, you will probably find a turning ring near the centre which – with a combination of luck and some reasonable wrist power – should enable you to fix the 'mike' at about six inches below the level of your mouth. Position the microphone carefully, even if this means keeping people waiting while you adjust the cord, or, if at a table, while it gets lifted over the wine and whisky. Once the position and the level are right and the microphone is switched on, check for volume. Talk into it. Ask, if you wish: 'Can you hear me?' but do not tap or bash the mouthpiece.

You should be able to stand (or, in some cases, sit) comfortably and six inches away from the microphone and still have your voice come through loud, clear and undistorted. If there is a scream, pop, whistle or shriek, it is too loud; if a whisper, too soft. If your voice sounds as if it comes from outer space, with Martian echo or eerie ululation, then something needs adjusting.

You may be given a neck microphone. The engineers will adjust it for sound and level.

With luck and perseverance, the microphone will be put into proper order. If it is not, or if the reception is intermittent or unpleasant, then you must make up your mind as to whether or not your voice will carry. Is it better to risk being unheard than to submit your audience to squeals and screeches from the machine? Think on your feet – fast – and stay calm.

'Are you receiving me?' you might say. 'Can you hear me at the back?' Your audience may laugh but note: they are laughing *with* you and not at you. You have command of the situation. You are waiting until the conditions are as you wish them to be before you start speaking. One way or another, you are off – even if it is to a late and slightly unhappy start. Your audience has seen that you have complete confidence. More good speeches are ruined because speakers are not prepared to take their time and make their pitches or other presentations with the microphone than for almost any other reason.

Once you are speaking into a fixed microphone, you are limited in your movement. When you shift away from the mouthpiece, the volume falls; turn your head either way and your words may be addressed to the entire hall but will he heard only by those at your feet. Find your distance from the machine and stay there. Within limits, you can relax, but move outside those limits and you are lost.

Lift an ordinary microphone off its stand, tuck your elbow into your side; make sure that there is plenty of 'play' in the cord – and walk, with the microphone always at the same distance from your mouth. If you use a neck or tie clip microphone, take care not to trip over the cord.

Beware of radio microphones. They pick up outside interference and sometimes hit dead spots.

Experience will show you how best to make use of the microphone. Never panic when the amplifier goes wrong. Be prepared to fall back on your own voice power, if you have to – so that you are not afraid of the microphone giving out.

Part 4

TECHNIQUES AT THE PITCH – HOW TO WIN

39

Team Work

Pitches are judged by overall impression. Each individual contributes; any individual can destroy; but ultimately, it is the team effect which is the deciding factor.

The scene is set from the Chair. Control, atmosphere and the central impression emerge from the centre and radiate outwards.

The client wants a company that is in control. If, as the pitcher, your act is individual and not collective, you won't win. So look up and be attentive, take physical note of what colleagues are saying and do not forget to refer to them when you speak: for example, 'John was right to say that . . .' or 'I would like to emphasize immediately Mary's most important point, that we . . .'

Try to avoid clichés like 'So over to you, Joan . . .' or 'So, without further ado – Bill – go for it!'

While presenting, keep referring back: 'As John said . . .' or 'Let me add to what Michael has told you . . .', but not 'I'm not going to bore you by repeating what Jack has said . . .'

Use new words, bright phrases, lively ideas – and feed them, back and forward, passing the ball like good footballers. By working together as a team, you will not only cope with the expected, but deal with – or even take advantage of – sudden events or opportunities. Remember the classic and moving World War II story of the famous comedian, Jimmy Durante. The producer, Ed Sullivan, touring veterans' hospitals with Durante warned his friend: 'No encores, Jimmy. We must be on the plane at 10.30 sharp.'

When the time came to leave, Ed saw Jimmy doing an encore and he beckoned him from behind the curtain: 'Hey, Jimmy, get off that stage. There's no encores.'

'Sorry, Ed,' said Jimmy, 'I can't leave. Look at that pair of soldiers clapping in the second row.' There sat two men, each of whom had lost one arm, clapping together with their remaining arms.

Join your talents, work together and, whatever your handicaps, you will deserve to win.

40

Chairing

If you are in the Chair, consider the following:

- The success or failure of the pitch will depend to a major extent on the impression that you personally make on your audience.
- You must accept the responsibility for ensuring that your preparation – and that of your colleagues and of your case – is full and adequate. Delegation is your privilege, responsibility and burden.
- If you do not control your team in its pitch, your audience will have no faith in your control of your organization, or in your ability to provide the services or goods that you are inviting them to buy.
- It is your job to see that your team 'gets its act together'. If they give different answers to the same questions, argue with each other instead of discussing with the judges, or do not put forward the same proposals or propositions – it is your fault. You must field the questions and pass them across to the appropriate players. You must ensure that they – and you – know in advance how to deal with difficult questions – on price, for example (see Chapter 44).
- If you chair the presentation, someone else will be in charge of its audience. Try to discuss with him or her, and in advance, the format of the event. The more that its actual running is left to you, the better – provided, of course, that you have worked out how best to produce the results you require.
- Consider whether you prefer to take questions during the course of individual talks, etc.; or after each; or at the end.
- Whatever you decide in advance be prepared to alter course if the unexpected occurs – which it always will, especially if you are not prepared for it.

- Make sure that all the members of your team are trained in presentation work.
- Remember, others will be pleased to share in your glory if you succeed, but – as Chair – you will be welcome to the entire blame if the presentation goes wrong.
- In the famous words of Harry Truman, 'If you don't like the heat, get out of the kitchen'. As Chair, you are both kitchen planner and chief cook. You may leave the bottle washing to others, but you are personally responsible for breakages. If you do not like responsibility, get out of the Chair. And do not ruin the work of your colleagues through failure in your own command – of yourself, of them, or of the presentation itself.

41

Offstage

When you pitch, you are never offstage – not even while other team members are performing.

Watch any team discussion on television and, with luck, you will see inexperienced participants making fools of themselves when they think that the camera is on someone else – smirking, yawning, showing inattention or whatever.

Teaching MPs to cope with the newly televised Chamber, a colleague and I taught them the rules of 'the doughnut' – that area around the speaker which is so often on screen: fill your doughnut so that the box does not show you in an empty chamber, and if you are in the doughnut for others, pay attention, look interested and show your agreement.

As in the Commons, so in pitches – you are never offstage. This means you must:

- Always look interested while your companions are talking.
- Show agreement, in sensible moderation.
- Show appreciation, amusement or other sensible reactions to colleagues' points.
- Be prepared to provide back up – passing helpful notes, binding documents in bundles or showing quiet attention to items which may provide answers to awkward questions.
- Be prepared to help out by answering questions, if your colleague turns to you for assistance.

Do *not*:

- Obviously worry about your own forthcoming contribution while colleagues are making theirs.
- Look down at your notes for your presentation, instead of looking up at the current presenter.
- Cough, scratch, wriggle, fiddle, clap, jingle or otherwise distract.

- Twist your hair, prod your ear, pick your nose or engage in any other nervous habits so unpleasant to observe.
- Interrupt without invitation.
- Argue, dispute or disagree with a colleague's point.

Above all, remember that when you are pitching, you must never lower your guard. Concentrate all the time.

42

Difficult Customers

We were training a group of four professionals. Three were keen, interested, lively, involved and amusing. The fourth sat, glaring grimly; refusing to take any part in the activity; answering in monosyllables. He obviously had not wanted to come, although he claimed to have volunteered. He would clearly have done better to go, although he insisted that he wished to stay. Result: we had to steer the course around him and do our best.

As a student of juvenile delinquency I was taught a little about the handling of aggressive people. You do not respond with aggression. You absorb hostility; keep your cool, your calm and your good nature. Eventually (you hope) they will respond. 'It's all done by love,' the tutor once told me.

With great restraint, then, my colleague trainer and I turned our other cheeks and returned concern for rudeness. Nothing worked on him, but his colleagues made it plain that they did not blame us; they were on our side; they benefitted from the days; and they saw to it that he was isolated and that we continued to work for the company.

Rule one in dealing with such people is to keep your cool and your courtesy.

Rule two is equally important: never be cowed by a bully.

I know many tycoons. Most have had their ruthless moments while treading their way up to the top, but once there, they relax. Any hostility is likely to be addressed to others at their own level. Many are wonderfully courteous to their juniors, and usually to those who seek their custom or help.

There are, of course, exceptions – people who actually enjoy being rude to you, not necessarily out of any malice but sometimes to see how you react and stand up to them; sometimes, just for fun.

Bend your neck before one of these people and you are finished. Hold your head, eyes and voice up – and always respond with courtesy. You may not win the pitch, but at least you will keep your self-respect and will probably win the respect of your persecutor. Start shouting, and your case is done for and so are you.

Watch out for the experienced and cunning questioner, who destroys by sneer or by insinuation, or even by tone of voice. Find out in advance as much as you can about your judges and their likely behaviour, and plan how to respond.

If you are up against someone who does not equate your case with you and who has a personal and emotional dislike for both, look to your weapons, or get someone else to do the pitch for you. In particular, hope that this person will not be the one who 'holds the butter'.

As always, knowing and preparing your case must have top priority. Unlike the exam student who prepares at reasonable leisure and faces the ordeal, with other victims, in the individual solitude of the silent exam room, you are likely ᴛo have little time for preparation and your examination will be very public.

Whatever your dislike for your questioner, try not to show it. The more unpleasant they are to you, the cooler and the more courteous you should become. In a confrontation, you must make your opponent's task as difficult as possible. Curiously, this is often best achieved through damning their faint praise or praising with faint damns, for example: 'I have always regarded your company as one of the highest repute . . . so it is really very difficult to understand how you could now . . .' or 'Well, you are an old hand at this game – and you will forgive me if I do not fall into that trap! The truth is that . . .'

If this approach is used against you, say something like, 'I appreciate Mr Black's backhanded compliment – these days, any sort of compliment given to an . . . is too rare to be rejected. So let's accept that I am an expert . . . that I do understand the situation/industry/profession as well as he says. Then that lends weight to my view, which is . . .'

Now for dodging the 'dirty' question. If you are in court and you deflect a question without answering it, the judge is liable to intervene with 'Please *do* answer the question, Mr Brown'.

Similarly, a questioner at a beauty contest may protest: 'But Mr Brown, you still have not told us. . . .' Or he or she may keep hammering: 'I think you should answer my question frankly – unless, of course, you would rather not. . . .' Reply firmly: 'I am sure it's my fault, but I thought that I had explained that point. Let me try again, please . . .' or 'Thank you for emphasizing that point – I obviously did not make it clear before. So let me try putting it a different way. . . .'

Always answer questions directly if you can. If not, provide an answer that is both true and acceptable. But parry the thrust if you must: 'Our annual return shows a gross profit of . . .' Then qualify the answer: 'But we had to transfer an exceptionally heavy amount to. . . .'

If silence is the best answer, deflect: 'Compared to other companies in the same business, our mark-up is low, and what matters to you is the cost-effective service we shall provide, especially bearing in mind that. . . .' To shift attention, always bear something else in mind!

A good questioner will ask a question and let the victim get on with answering it. Some questioners are not so good, and most victims do not answer.

If you regard an interruption as unfair, then stop – do not be bullied. Say 'May I finish my sentence, please' or 'If you don't mind, I will finish this point and then move onto your question. . . .' Then wrap up your point as swiftly as you can.

The more powerful your interrogator, or the more obnoxious, the more likely it is that he or she will despise you if you show any sign of fear. To win the work, you must command respect. So stand up to the questioning, courteously but firmly.

If you are asked a difficult question, consider its source. It is not only at political meetings that questions are often asked so that the speaker will give an answer that can be used by the questioner against mutual opponents, or so that the doubter in the same audience may perhaps be convinced.

As always, concentrate: do not allow your attention to be distracted for a moment. The more fierce the questioning, the greater your concentration must be. Some other useful ripostes are:

'I wonder whether it is really the right moment to answer that question. . . ?'

'I would be very glad to look into the matter you have raised – but surely, it would be better done privately, wouldn't it?'

'We do not consider that progress could be made, until. . . .'

'It shouldn't be long before we could usefully discuss that point – but it will take some careful consideration. . . .'

'I am sorry. I really must insist that we do not reveal that information at this stage in our discussions. . . .'

Preserve other people's confidentiality and your judge will know that you will respect theirs.

Never walk out: if you break off relations, you will certainly lose. Remember Oscar Wilde explaining that whenever he felt the inclination to take exercise, he would lie down until it passed off. If you feel the inclination to walk out, take a deep breath and hold it, until that inclination passes off!

Finally, if you do not really mind losing the pitch but you prefer to leave with your dignity intact, then retort with crushing wit. But make sure that you at least win the battle with your judges.

43

Politics

A nasty business, politics, isn't it? MPs attacking each other and using every dirty trick to win power and elections? You wouldn't run into that in business or a profession, would you? Not much, you wouldn't – and never more than when angry rivals are competing for the same carcass. The political jungle is not the sole habitat of politicians.

Former Canadian Prime Minister, Lester Pearson, described politics as 'the skilled use of blunt objects'. Watch out for your judges. They will be using blunt objects and you must see that they do not land on your skull.

As a start, try to find out as much as you can in advance about those who will face you across the table. This (once again) includes: who holds the butter? And also, who wants to hold it? Who would be better off if you won and why? Whose power would increase if you lost, and for what reason? Whose back would be better protected if a particular opponent gets appointed? Who would feel more secure under your wing, and in what circumstances?

Politics is the art of government. It is the method by which any organization, national or local, commercial or professional, is run. People want power in order to achieve results – which may be in the form of personal promotion or a corporate restructure, an individual ambition or a company acquisition.

So when asking 'Who?', it is not enough simply to study the corporate image or structure, needs or attributes, products or services of your quarry. You must look at the politics. If you want to work *with* your judges, you must at least understand their political motivation.

If, for instance, you are pitching to a public authority, national or local, you must contend with both variables and invariables. Are you dealing with paid officials or with elected members? Or both? The officials will probably and reasonably be more interested in protecting their backs than the elected people, but even that cannot be guaranteed. Officials want to keep their offices and the elected need to win elections. How will you help each to achieve those objectives? Both are servants of their electorate. Each must be a political animal. Recognize that interest and you deserve to win; ignore it at your peril.

Now take the not uncommon case of the heads of divisions, large or small, who actually hate the people at the top, possibly because the mighty starve those divisions or individuals of the resources they need. A normal divisional reaction is to block, if they can, spending plans desired by the centre, unless those plans provide specific benefit for the divisions. Any pitch would have to take such factors into account.

When you plan your strategy and your tactics, then, you must do so remembering that politics, by definition, means government. People wish to govern so as to put their own ideas into effect, hopefully for the benefit of the community but (not least in business) often so that they may have the pleasure of governing. Don't despise it: just as you will work to retain that power in your own business, you must expect others to do so in theirs.

Your judges may, of course, be blessed with unanimity of purpose, in which case you can get on with your job of beating your opponents. If, though, your judges are busy trying to beat each other, then they will be looking at the contestants to find out who is most likely to promote their point of view, their ideas, their products, their services, their division of the company, their power base, etc.

Recognizing the politics, the problems and the people, you must then apply your own political cunning. There are two main alternatives. Like the renowned Vicar of Bray, you can try to please all parties, preparing to ride whatever horse is available and to stay in the saddle whatever occurs. You may do so in ways that are devious, or you may simply plough on, ignoring the whims and declining to trim your sails.

The other alternative is to aim your presentation at the interests of one side.

When dealing with public authorities, local or national, it should not be too difficult to sort out the politics in advance. In other cases, you may have to wait until you get there. Sometimes, though, you will have no way of knowing, and you will have to be especially careful to keep eye contact, sharpen your antennae and observe audience reaction to what you and your colleagues say. That is the real test of the professional. It means thinking on your feet and reacting without warning.

All this should form part of your planning and rehearsal. If the pitch is important, you should prepare your approach, your reactions and your answers to questions, based on the varied reactions that you meet. But watch out for bluff and double bluff: your judges' reactions may be based on their own efforts to probe, their questions designed to lead you into traps by indicating a leaning in one direction when in reality it goes in another. Remember the classic tale of the pitcher who was asked by one man, 'Do you agree with me?' 'Yes you are right', replied the pitcher. A man with a contrary view then asked him the same question. 'Yes, I agree,' said the pitcher again. A third man then said, 'You can't possibly agree with two opposite views, can you?' 'You are also right,' said the pitcher!

If you want to be elected to office, it's a good rule to keep in with the majority of your electors. In a pitch, though, there is no such joy as one person, one vote – one person may hold all the votes. Identify him or (too occasionally) her. Keep in with the mogul or you are out.

Another important political rule: you can fall out with those who are not going to vote for you anyway, but if you lose your own supporters, you are finished. You will not find any party too busy at election time wooing the homeless or spending too much time with Jehovah's Witnesses, or with others who could vote but don't. However much you may search for allies among your apparent opponents, it is rarely wise to do so at the expense of your natural supporters. It is scarcely a compliment to be described as a 'politician'.

It is a compliment, though, to be described as 'politic'. This suggests an intelligent appreciation of the sensitivities of others. In pitching, you need a politic approach to the politics of your quarry.

Political elections are major pitches to the public. Beauty contests are elections, won by the first past the post. If you want to win, get the politics right.

44

Fees and Prices

Professional people charge different fees; business people, varying prices. Professions and businesses often overlap, in the services and products they provide; and both fees and prices are usually both negotiable and negotiated.

Bernard Shaw once said to Sam Goldwyn, when refusing to sell him the screen rights to his plays: 'The trouble, Mr Goldwyn, is that you are only interested in art and I am only interested in money!' There is an art to earning money through beauty contests. It starts with the recognition that all your monetary interest is matched by – and in some respects, contrary to – that of your quarry.

You must first decide what you are going to charge – and whether or not that charge is negotiable. Fixing your charge is a matter for your expertise, based on your assessment of what will be profitable to you. You must do what suits your business, and you may need different approaches for different parts of that business. The time to decide on any deals to be done is also before you get to your pitch. You and your team must discuss fees and prices and whether or not they are negotiable.

There are two basic rules on how not to get caught out over money. Rule One is to be positive. Do not shy away from financial questions. Your quarry are entitled to ask and to expect you to answer them clearly. Professional people are especially prone to money shyness – a hangover from the old cricketing days when things were divided into 'gentlemen' and 'players'. Lawyers, accountants, surveyors, architects and the rest were all 'gentlemen', who preferred to leave money discussions to others – or who, at least, did not believe that money should be discussed other than by consenting partners in private. Today, however, frankness on fees is an essential.

If you make a living at least partly because your fees or prices are competitive – say so. When challenged, do not back off. For example, if a client says: 'Mr Brown, your fees are much higher than some of the other companies which have pitched for this contract. What do you say to that?' don't reply with, 'Well, I wonder whether that is correct? We don't reckon to charge more than most people. What do you think, Joe?' Joe: 'Yes, I think that is right. I would be glad to consider any examples you would give us of fees which you thought were too high,' or 'I'm sorry, but we don't really like to discuss fees at this stage.'

Such replies are defensive, unsatisfactory – and far too typical. Try instead, 'Our charges/prices are competitive, and certainly thoroughly cost-effective. After all, what matters to our clients/customers is that they end up by paying for having the job done/the product produced in an entirely satisfactory way' or, 'Yes, we are at the top of the market. But then we provide a top service – which is why our business has doubled in the past . . . years.'

Emphasize that your customers or clients are well satisfied, and that your prices or fees are cost-effective. Above all, *do not apologize*, directly or indirectly, by words or by implication.

Basic Rule Two on not getting caught out over money is to decide on your approach in advance and never be trapped into arguing about it as follows:

'So those are your fees, Mr Brown. Are they negotiable?'

Mr Brown: 'No, sir.'

'Surely if we provide you with a large enough contract, you would be prepared to negotiate, wouldn't you? Mr Brown, what do you say to that?'

Mr Brown: 'Well, I suppose if it is large enough, we would be prepared to discuss a discount.'

Result – disaster.

Get everything else right but mess up your approach to fees or charges and you lose. Be positive, clear and provably cost-effective, and you deserve to win.

45

Conflicts of Interest and Chinese Walls

To represent one client, one interest, one side in a battle, is fair, reasonable and honest. To represent differing interests brings you into conflict. Potential clients or customers will wish to know in advance how you will handle conflicts if, as, and when they arise.

First, consider how conflicts arise and are dealt with in practice. There are many possibilities. The first is the so-called 'Chinese Wall'.

Suppose, for instance, that two clients of the same bank are involved in a takeover battle. Each may be handled by a different team, department or individual within the bank. They will build between themselves what they will describe as a 'Chinese Wall' – a barrier that is invisible, but intended to be real. Its foundations are laid in integrity. Hopefully, the wall and those who build it will be equally upright.

Chinese Walls are normally operated by suppliers of services. They make it possible to retain the goodwill and (let's face it) the money of both parties. Their limits are obvious. For instance, you can hardly build one in your own mind, so if confidential information may actually or potentially reach your mind or that of any other person in your firm, you cannot block it out. You may separate departments but not the lobes of your business brain.

Clients sometimes treat Chinese Walls with suspicion, merited or otherwise: 'I don't see how you lot can serve two masters . . . you'd better make up your minds.' Or there may be a leak, which has nothing whatever to do with the Chinese Wall. But suspicion lurks.

In *How to Read the Financial Pages* (Hutchinson Business Books, 1989) Michael Brett writes that Chinese Walls are 'barriers that are supposed to exist between different arms of a securities house to prevent information from passing between them. Sometimes they are invisible walls. Sometimes the different arms are physically separated. Cynics claim that they have never met a Chinese Wall that did not have a grapevine growing over it'. Indeed.

Option One, then, is to carry whichever passengers will pay, keeping them in separate vehicles. Option Two is to turn down one fare or the other – the problem is, which one?

In practice, you have to ask yourself who you would least wish to offend, upset or risk losing. After all, on the assumption that competitors are pleased with your services, the ones you dump are unlikely to be flattered. They may find a reliable alternative whom they prefer and with whom they stay.

You could decide on the 'first come, first served' basis. Two clients are competing for a job? One of them has booked your services? Then if the other turns to you later, that will be too late.

If one client comes to you and you know that the other is likely to be interested, you cannot tell the other because that would be breaking a confidence with the first. Or perhaps when the second one finds out that you knew but did not report, the action may not be favourable.

Option One is to have both. Option Two is to reject one or other. Option Three is to reject both: scarcely a profitable arrangement in the short run, but sometimes a long-term investment in the trust of both parties.

With all these possibilities clearly in view, you should be able to approach your beauty parade with firm and agreed answers to the following questions:

'If we take on your services/accept your proposition/buy your product, will you give us exclusivity? Can we rely on you not to act for/sell to competitors?'

'If we find ourselves in competition against another of your clients, will we be able to rely on you to honour your obligations to us – or will you be shooting off?'

Be sure to work out your answers before the questions are asked.

Part 5

SPECIAL TARGET OCCASIONS AND AUDIENCES

46

Handling Large Audiences

Many brilliant performers on stage and platform shrivel up and bore in the intimacy of close-up presentations. They happily project from afar, radiating personality but, when they come near, display a positive dislike for eye and emotional contact.

Most business people, however, manage at least adequately with a few listeners, but dread the large audience. Most pitching is done to small groups, so they survive intact. When they get thrown before an assembly, they freeze with terror and do minimal justice to themselves and their case.

You may, for instance, have to address a conference. Conferences do not provide pitching opportunities in the ordinary sense, but they are your shop window. You should therefore invest time, resources and variety in conference or seminar presentations.

One way or another, you will have to know how to persuade and win beyond the intimacy of the private office or boardroom.

The simplest and most important rule for dealing with a large audience is – treat it as if it were a small one. That means:

- Be yourself. Do not change your personality. Chat. It is a grave, and almost universal, error to believe that when the audience grows, you must alter your style. Change your techniques, yes, but yourself, your personality, your approach – never.
- Eye contact is vital. If you do not watch your audience, you can neither make nor maintain contact with them. You cannot react to them, nor see how they are reacting to you.

  Start with your eyes on someone friendly, in or near the centre of the audience and not too far back. Then move your eyes, stopping for about five seconds in each position. Eye movement means neck movement: swivel your eyes and you will look like a snake; necks are for turning.

Imagine that you are driving your car. You may travel quite a distance, thinking of something other than the road (which is not recommended, but which happens) so that after you have covered that distance, you say to yourself, 'How did I get here?' The answer is: experience and conditioned reactions. Your eyes are on the road so that if an unusual event occurs, you will snap to attention. If (for instance) a child comes out from in front of a car, 50 yards away, you will see him or her.

If you take your eyes off the road, though, you – and the child – may be killed.

As when driving a car, so when steering an audience. Watch them all the time. Once used to the system – look, turn, look, turn – you will notice audience reactions, even when you are not looking at the individuals.

When addressing an audience of about a hundred, I will notice if two at the back start talking, if someone yawns, and above all, if any individuals or sections of the audience start to shift in their seats.

Of course, you cannot do any of this if your eyes are on a script. Eye contact with paper may be necessary, but it should be kept to the minimum. Read directly from notes only if you really must (see Chapter 31).

'Plant' questions to help you break the ice when you hit Question Time, and make sure you get the ones you want.

If you are greeted with silence – probably because the Chair failed to induce or to start the clapping – a good opening gambit is to smile and say, 'Thank you . . . very much . . . for that enthusiastic welcome!'

At the end of a speech to a large audience, it helps to have what opera singers call a 'claque' – one or two people to get the applause moving and to create the feel of satisfaction and success, the atmosphere of winning.

The basic principles of pitching to a large audience are as follows:

- Silence. Use it. Don't be afraid to pause . . . to give your audience breathing, thinking, shifting time. Too many presenters are scared to give a large audience time to adjust – to ideas and to positions.
- Involve. Don't feel that, because an audience is large, you can't (for instance) ask them questions.

   I almost always start with a question – often rhetorical, such as 'I wonder how many of you have to deal with this situation?' Or 'Is there anyone here who has not had to cope with. . . ?' (See also Chapter 26.)

- Recognize individuals. A large audience is simply a gathering of individual people. Our slogan for teaching presentation is 'We train individuals in groups, not groups of individuals'.
- Recognize individuality and play up to it. Pick out senior people and refer to them: 'Mrs White is here, an expert at. . . . Where are you, Mrs White? I wonder whether you would care to comment on what I have just said?'
- Be heard. Lift up your voice. Or, as my old, and rather deaf, national law tutor at Harvard used to bellow at us: 'Take your voice . . . throw it against the back wall . . . and make it b-o-u-n-c-e . . . off!' For rules on voice production, see Chapter 17. If you need to use a microphone, follow those in Chapter 38.

  Don't assume that you are speaking audibly – ask, 'Can you hear me at the back?' Or place your spouse or some other outspoken personage at the back. My wife needs no invitation to sing out: 'Speak up!' Or she merely stands and holds her cupped hands behind her ears!
- Body language. Stand up, lift up your head and your chin. Throw back your shoulders, so that you can clearly project your voice.

  Look as confident as you wish to feel and your confidence will soon emerge.

47

Conferences and Seminars

Most of this book deals with the direct pitch – the one where you are competing for specific work from known clients. But there is also the shop window – the conference or seminar, organized by yourselves or others.

Whatever form the event takes, it is a promotional exercise and an indirect pitch. It may be designed to introduce new clients or to strengthen the loyalty of old ones – either way, you are in show business. However dull the subject, you should try to enliven it with wit (Chapter 28) and visual aids (Part 3) and bring it to life with the three Es – Energy, Enthusiasm and Excitement.

Individual speakers should follow the rules of presentation. In particular, they should know and prepare their material; communicate with, and according to, their audiences; speak with style and demonstrate with skill.

Whether dealing with a small-scale teaching seminar or a larger assembly or conference, excellent presenters respect their audiences and entertain them. The fact that so many conferences are dull and disastrous is a denunciation of those who organize and address them. They not only harm their own cause, but also spoil the market. They forget that while schoolchildren are tied to their desks and to their classrooms, conference delegates can opt for the bar.

Presenters' success depends to a vast extent, however, on the conditions created for them by the conference or seminar organizers. Check these in advance, preferably before you agree to take part. If, for instance, the room is to be vast and the audience small, the acoustics echoing and the amplification minimal, the delegates crowded and unhappy, and the food inedible – then do not attach your company's good name to their bad feelings.

If you do go, arrive early enough to check your atmosphere and your apparatus, your audience and your audibility. Pay special regard to the following:

- Is the stage, platform and/or table as you like or need it?
- Stuck as *you* are with the amplification arrangements as *they* are, how can you make the best of them? For instance, will you be able to remove, adjust and/or stroll with the microphone, or is it fixed?
- Is the overhead projector or other equipment for your visual aids in proper order and position? If you need assistance with, say, the showing of slides, is it available?
- If you need particular arrangements for your comfort and convenience, such as water for a dry throat, will you get them? Is there provision of pre-meal drinks or intermission tea or coffee?
- If you are to be paid a fee for your presentation, are the arrangements clear, recorded or confirmed in writing and followed through? If these are to any extent on a commission, bonus or other arrangement that depends upon the success of the event, then how will you find out what you are owed; and will you need to send an account or invoice?
- Should you require smokers to remain at the back or to one side, or will you mix the chimneys with the abstainers? Or can you prohibit smoking?
- Always try to fill up seats from the front. If you are not sure whether the room will be filled, try to make sure that no one sits in the back rows until front and centre are full.
- If you are to be introduced by a Chair or other impresario, has he or she adequate and correct details for the purpose? Have you arranged for details, samples, order forms, brochures or other documents to be properly and prominently displayed?
- Try to avoid interruptions from the clatter of crockery and cutlery before and after breaks. Separate reception and coffee rooms will help, but thin partitions destroy the best of plans.

48

One-to-One and Round the Table

At the opposite end of the presentational scale to a large audience comes a task which is equally formidable – the one-to-one, eyeball-to-eyeball, individual competitive sell.

Far from ducking into the decent darkness of a 35 mm slide show, or even losing your fears in the crowd (yes, that's how some veteran performers actually feel), you are faced with your quarry – literally.

You are being watched. So borrow some of the magician's techniques. There's 'misdirection', for instance: the conjuror moves his hand and watches his fingers – the watcher's eyes will automatically follow.

Close-up, your movements and your eyes are as important as they would be if you were on a television screen. Keep your eyes on the other person. That doesn't mean staring or even a constant gaze, but looking your quarry in the eyes and not letting yours go glazed.

Your quarry will be assessing you and your offerings and observing your movements. So move with economy and deliberation, recognizing that whether it is your eyes or your body that's shifting, that's a language of its own.

How far can or should you use visuals, when presenting around a table? You should supplement sound with sight and hearing with vision whenever that will add to, and not detract from, your presentation. But the method is different when you are on your seat instead of your feet.

There's nothing to stop you saying to your audience: 'Now, forgive me for a moment. I am going to stand up and show you some pictures of . . .' Up you get and on go the 35 mms. It provides a break, variety, extra life.

You might like to put examples of your product onto the table. Pass them round, or, if appropriate, give one to each participant.

The prepared flipovers designed for table display are fine if you are showing samples of cloth or of carpet, but we would not recommend them for sophisticated services. As we've seen them used by bankers, stockbrokers or lawyers, they somehow look cheap, however slick or expensive they may be.

Documentation is usually better. Use it according to its nature and whether or not it has been sent out and read in advance.

The less – or the less lively – the visuals, the more important – and the livelier – you must make the presentation itself. Variety matters. 'The ayes have it', says Mr Speaker in the House of Commons, proclaiming the winner. If the eyes haven't got it, then you'd better get it right, through the ears.

The most sensitive pitches are those made individually and personally. You may feel uncomfortable if you try to sell on an aircraft, but comfort in times of sharp competition is an outdated luxury. So consider the presentation to the close-up contact, wherever found.

It may be undignified to ask for work, but it is far more so to be unable to pay your debts – or to be unemployed. Casual contacts will not resent being turned into customers or clients, provided that they get value for money. Here are some suggestions:

- To strike up a relationship with fellow travellers, and to turn acquaintances into friends, look for their interests. They may advertise these through a tie, a badge, luggage labels, the obvious contents of hand luggage, or the correspondence that you cannot help seeing because the victim lays it out before you – if not deliberately, at least with no attempt to hide it.
- Your company should pay for first, business, executive or club class travel for your comfort, but also because you will share it with others at your commercial level. So will those of your fellow travellers. If they may be prospects for you, so you may be for them – mutual curiosity has promoted many a joint business venture.
- The interests of worthwhile contacts will include their business or professional concerns. So once you have enquired about theirs, they may reasonably ask about yours. Your questions will have begun as innocently as comments about the weather and will shade from one subject into the next.
- If your approaches go wrong, you can always shrug and switch off: termination of an aircraft conversation can usually be achieved with a sigh and murmur that it is time to sleep. Saying 'I must get some work done, I'm afraid' can also serve as an indication of diligence, making you worthy of some future fee.

- Always carry business cards, especially in Japan and the East. A smart and legible business card is essential to courteous introduction and future contact. An exchange of cards is an invitation to keep in touch: give generously and collect avidly.
- Mealtimes are best for chatting – the thread of conversation may easily weave into the cloth of commerce.
- Like seeks like and trades with it. Obviously, the more likeable you appear and the more mutually interesting your ventures, the more joint they are likely to become.
- I once asked a distinguished statesman how he maintained such happy personal friendships with so many rulers, in so many diverse places. He replied: 'Because I talk family, music, theatre, sport . . . and then turn to politics. The personal word leads to the political as well as to the personal friendship – and the transfer of this worthy tactic of politics to business is entirely appropriate.'

You may begin by selling to your prospects – and end by buying from them. Good luck to you both.

49

Mealtime Selling

I asked one of the UK's most successful sellers of financial services: 'What do you do at your beauty contest?' He replied: 'We eat!'

Dining tables are some of the world's finest pitching grounds. Using them requires special techniques, preparation and care.

When you are dealing with small groups and specific mealtime pitches, attenders and placing are crucial. Who will come from your outfit and whom should you ask from your clients? Will they decide on numbers and choose their participants or should you issue specific invitations?

If the pitch is indirect, why not consider inviting one of your satisfied clients, who may do more to sell your services than your own modesty would permit?

Always check whether any of your guests have specific dietary requirements. Vegetarian, kosher or halal, perhaps?

The intimate mealtime pitch is a relaxed form of meeting, designed for informality. As a mealtime presenter, you join the ranks of the cabaret artiste. Ask successful performers in that most complex craft and they will explain the pitfalls. For instance, instead of having your audience in front of you, with their bodies and their heads hopefully turned in your direction, they will be scattered and clumped around tables, eyes and minds concentrated on plates and glasses. Some may turn their heads, their bodies, or even their chairs, so as to watch you; others will allow your voice to go in one ear and out the other, without allowing their eyesight to interfere with their hearing.

So, keep the lights on and your presentation lively and varied. If possible, use a roving microphone. Place yourself wherever most people can see you with the least discomfort – whether that be at the front, at the side or in the middle. If there is a platform – for the band or for the top table – use it. If there is none, and you want one, ask for one.

If possible, work out your routine beforehand and co-ordinate arrangements with the Master of Ceremonies, Chair or toastmaster. If you *organize* a mealtime occasion to be preceded or followed by a presentation, please bear the presenter's problems most carefully in mind. Indeed, if you are the provider of the banquet, check in advance how best to ease the presenter's task. Use the above notes as a checklist and then consider the following:

- As with all gatherings, a few people packed into a small room should help to produce success; but a large audience half filling a vast area is the surest guarantee of failure. If in doubt, pack them in. If necessary, use partitions.
- Select your top targets and ensure that they are well seated. If in doubt about their preferences, enquire: 'Would you prefer to be at the top table or with the French Ambassador/Board of Directors (or as the case may be)?' Human dignity is never more vulnerable than when its bearers are on public view. Those who consider themselves separated from the great – either by too great a distance or none at all – may leave before the presentation begins. Or if they are physically present, their minds will be concentrated on revenge.
- If you must have a top table, then perhaps it should be a round one, in the centre of the room, so that far more people may feel that they are close to it. Or maybe you could have a director to host each table?
- Beware of rushing. Allow for those without whom you cannot sit down to be reasonably late – then insist that the banquet begins as near as possible to the precisely planned minute.
- If time is short and the presentation crucial, use guile to reduce the time taken by the meal. Did you know that you can cut meal times by about ten minutes if you serve fish or meat *off* the bone, rather than leaving your guests to fiddle for ages with, for instance, the carcass of a capon or a calf? You could also serve the coffee immediately after the main course, together with the dessert, to save time.
- Consider breaking up the presentation. For instance, maybe someone should speak to your guests before the meal? Be careful with this, however: I once attended an Indian banquet with 12 speeches before the meal was served. Our mood was not improved by the extreme spiciness of the Madras curry that followed!

50

The Telephone

Before or after your pitch, you will probably have to speak to your prospect by telephone. Your smile may be radiant, your personality magnetic, and your appearance may create the perfect image for your purpose, but if your voice is flat, your telephone presentation will land on its back. Yet telephone technique is rarely taught, even to people whose livelihood depends upon it. They are expected to cope through trial and error.

This chapter is designed to minimize your telephonic trials and errors alike, and to help you to make the best of that inevitably massive percentage of working time which you and your colleagues will spend presenting and persuading by telephone.

Let's start with the voice. Begin by recording your voice and playing it back, then ask yourself the following questions:

- Am I conveying charm? It takes no more time to be charming than it does to appear boring or bored, patronizing or proud, disinterested or uninteresting.
- Do I sound confident? If you sound timid, hesitant or not in command of yourself, your material, your subject or your intentions, then you can only lose. (It is far easier to feign self-confidence in person when you can look your prospect, customer or client straight in the eye, than it is by telephone).
- Do I sound enthusiastic? Whatever you are trying to convey, you should do so with vocal verve and energy.
- Does my voice convey variety – or am I one of those natural telephonic disasters who provide (literally) monotony through monotone? Whatever the undoubted importance of varying your tone, delivery, speed and rhythm when on your feet, change is even more vital by telephone. The longer the call, the more crucial the variation.

Assume, now, that you modestly find some room for improvement in your telephone presentations. How can you best achieve this?

First, use your imagination. Forget that you are communicating by telephone. Seat your listener on the other side of your desk or table – and talk to him or her. Use the converse of television technique, where you normally speak to your interviewer and forget your audience. Imagine yourself in one of those oblique and terrifying studios where you can talk to a screen from which sometimes your own face stares back at you, and conjure up the vision of your victim, instead of allowing yourself to be his or hers. This is not hard when you know the person at the other end of the line. If you have trouble at first in adopting this technique, you could even put the person's photograph before you.

Then forget that you are talking to a machine. Smile and laugh; grimace and gesticulate; even exaggerate your facial and bodily responses; and you will find that these are automatically reflected in your voice. Use the techniques of the long-distance lover, who woos the telephone in his or her hand, leaving it to the person at the other end to translate voice into emotion.

Animate the receiver. Have you ever wondered why top-grade television stars, discussion leaders and communicators of all sorts, so often either hold or sit in front of microphones, when modern techniques could leave their hands free? By visibly holding the microphone, they instinctively carry a message to their audiences – wooing the microphone, and varying volume at their own will, instead of leaving it entirely to engineers or producers.

So use your receiver as a friend; and avoid, where you can, those awful machines that magnify sound. They are useful when, to the knowledge of the other parties, your voice must be conveyed to people other than you. But they provide an inhuman echo – a resonance that banishes the privacy that a telephone can, in theory at least, provide – and they make it doubly hard for you to project your charm, enthusiasm, confidence and persuasion to your listener.

If it is vital for someone to listen in at your end, then get an earphone attached to the receiver – but remember that others do the same. While you may record a conversation – literally 'for the record' or for whatever purpose – remember that bugs are impersonal objects, available to all.

Some time ago, I negotiated an arrangement with the editor of a local newspaper, to patch up a disagreement which arose entirely through my fault. I was to write a letter on agreed terms, which we hammered out by telephone.

'Fine,' I said at the end of our talk, 'I will write to you and confirm our conversation.'

'No need,' he replied, 'I have it on tape!'

It had not occurred to me that our conversation would be taped without my knowledge. I regarded it then, as I do now, as an invasion of the normal privacy of 'person to person' communication – and ever since, I have treated every telephone conversation as both open and recorded.

This rule, of course, has particular application to overseas telephone calls. If they are not recorded by your overseas communicant, they may be by several intelligence agencies.

So remember that when you speak by telephone, there may be others listening in – by chance, through a crossed line or, more likely, by intent. Your words may be recorded, and recorded evidence is generally admissible in court. Unrecorded calls are ephemeral. Any important conversation should be confirmed, immediately and in writing.

51

Foreign and Overseas

Pitching to foreigners? Then watch your language – and theirs.

Naturally, if you are fluent in the foreign language required, your problems are minimal: you only have to follow the rules in the rest of this book and all should be well. Subject, of course, to cutting your cloth to the style of your overseas audience, there is no essential difference between rousing, holding, interesting, convincing – or boring – an audience of English or French people, Russians or Greeks.

There are, however, some superficial differences. Melodrama goes over rather better in the United States than in Britain, for instance. The florid oratory that went out in Britain many years ago still thrives in parts – and with some audiences – abroad. In general, if you play up to the image expected of you – if you give your audience a touch of urbane wit, rather than roistering slapstick – you are likely to come across best.

A friend who made a massive success of selling to the Japanese offers the following rules:

- Treat Japanese people in exactly the opposite way to that which you would Americans.
- Never make a cold call. You are not only wasting your time but behaving in a way that is regarded as discourteous. Introductions, however spurious, are vital.
- Take all opportunities for introductions, however flimsy: 'I'm a friend of. . . .' 'It has been suggested to me by Mr . . . that I should contact you. . . .' 'We are especially pleased to be here because of our fondness for your friend, Mr. . . .'
- Japanese regard saying 'no' as rude. If they say 'We can see a number of difficulties', you're in trouble.
- The sucking in of breath is an indication of pleasure.
- If Japanese people do not understand what you are saying, they

will probably nod politely – so speak plainly. If they cannot hear what you are saying, they will not ask you to 'speak up'. Your words will simply be lost. So talk loudly and clearly.
● Above all, be patient.

Stick to your usual style when in America and you have every chance of a friendly welcome. I once toured the United States, talking about Britain. I met a certain surprise that this Englishman was not cold, reserved, humourless, upper crust and frosty. The image of the icy Anglo-Saxon who will only speak when introduced – and, preferably, when well warmed with alcohol – dies hard, so the friendly, humourous opening acquired an extra significance and importance. Establish a rapport and you are well away, you have warmed the house.

When pitching to people for whom English is not the mother tongue, you have two main options: either address them in English and hope that they will understand; or speak in the foreign language. The second is infinitely preferable, provided that you have sufficient command of the tongue concerned.

If you are really talking business – putting across facts, figures, theories or ideas in respect of which words must be given their precise meanings; if what you say may create misunderstandings if the words are not used with their correct nuances; if shades of meaning matter then you should stick to English and work through an interpreter if necessary (see Chapter 50). It is no tribute to your bravery to venture into foreign seas without a lifebelt.

On the other hand, there may be occasions when it would be worth preparing your pitch beforehand, having it translated – and then reading it. Make a friendly, impromptu opening (or one which is apparently not read) and the audience will just have to put up with what may not be an oratorical masterpiece but which will at least be accurate.

If you are making your presentation in English, you should always prepare a few words, right at the start, in your hosts' language – or, if you are the host, in that of your actual or potential customers or clients. It does not matter how badly you mispronounce the words – in fact it may add to the fun. Nobody cares if you make a hash of the grammar, or even if you manage to make a ghastly error which gives words their opposite meaning: what matters is that you make a genuine effort to speak in the relevant tongue. You pay the compliment of making what is obviously a brave attempt to be friendly – and in the most genuine possible way.

Start with your usual opening, in English: 'Ladies and Gentlemen, fellow workers in the. . . .' Then break into the foreign tongue – you will produce just that element of surprise which should give rise to a very friendly reception. Try to memorize something like the following in the foreign language:

'After I'd met Mr . . . in . . . who speaks such marvellous English, I was shamed into trying. I am only sorry that my efforts have been, as you hear, so very unsuccessful. To avoid any future misunderstandings of what I have to say, I hope that you will forgive me if I return – very gratefully – to English!'

If you really feel unable to memorize it, read it. The very fact that you have bothered to get the information and the translation from one of the nationals of the country concerned will undoubtedly be appreciated.

52

Interpreters and Translators

Interpreters are people who stand alongside and translate as you go along. The problem with it is that conversations take twice as long. The breaks for translation can also interrupt your train of thought.

There are advantages, however. Using an interpreter is inexpensive – you pay for the interpreter but not for equipment. This also gives you immediate access to conversation, with no delays for setting up equipment.

When dealing with an interpreter, the art is to speak slowly; and to pause often. Do not spew out quickly-spoken paragraphs, leaving your interpreter trailing behind.

You must pause after every few paragraphs, and especially after key points – to let the judges catch up with you. This also gives those of your audience who are not wearing the headphones and didn't need translation time to shift around in their seats.

Simultaneous translation is a skilled profession, but the translators need good sound and time to do their jobs. Time means – speak slowly. Good sound means – speak into the microphone and make sure that it is switched on. When a room is set out for simultaneous translation, you will normally need to press the button on your microphone, so that you get your sound through to the appropriate booth: no switch, no translation.

Both methods of translation may be irritating for listeners who did not need translation. For them, simultaneous is better because they can leave their headphones to one side and waste no time – the exception being those who prefer to hear something twice, the better to prepare their responses.

I learned this method from holocaust survivor Yossel Rosensaft. When I was a young soldier in the British Army of the Rhine and Yossel was Chairman of the Bergen Belsen Displaced Persons' Committee, I often sat in with him while he negotiated with British authorities over camp conditions. He spoke English admirably but preferred to work through an interpreter. The Control Commission officer understood Yossel's Yiddish only in translation, while Yossel absorbed the English both in its original and through the interpreter. Yossel and the officer were in competition, so time to think mattered.

53

Ten Ways Not to Answer

Ordinarily, you should always seek to answer fully any questions posed by your clients, actual or prospective. Sometimes, though, you may be faced with a question which it is impossible, for whatever reason, for you to answer. In such a case you must be able to avoid humiliation when evading the question. The following is a list of ways to avoid directly answering an unwanted question without seeming rude:

- Come clean and say that you do not know the answer, followed by 'But I'll find out for you and let you know . . .' or 'It's a very good question. I wonder if any of you can answer it?' or 'I'll get one of my colleagues to find the answer for you and will let you know. . . .'
- Say: 'That's an important question and I'm coming to that problem very shortly in the next part of my lecture/tomorrow morning. . . .' You then have two alternatives. You can and should 'come to it' – but you may not, in which case you must hope that your questioner will have forgotten it.
- Throw the question back to the questioner:'That's an important question. I wonder what view you and your collegues take of that matter? We have always found it a very difficult one to deal with.'
- Answer a different question. This is typical of politicians' answers: you supply information which you hope will satisfy the questioner, but avoid giving information which you either do not know or which you do not want to reveal.
- Refuse to answer. You will normally have to give some at least apparently acceptable reason, for instance, 'I'm sorry, but to answer that question would involve a breach of confidence' or 'Unfortunately, that is information which is really not mine to give'.

- Request that the question be discussed privately, for example, 'Mr Brown, that is a fair and a relevant question, but it is really one which might involve breach of confidentiality. If you wish to pursue it, would you please have a quiet word with me afterwards?'
- Refer the question to a committee. 'That is a very complex question. It would require additional research and if, as I hope, we do this job for you, I shall set up a special group to deal with that point and to report back to you on it in full.'
- Provide an apparent answer. Do so in a way that sounds plausible and real, and hope that the listeners will not recognize it as a non-answer. This may work, especially if you can deflect attention.
- Deflect attention. This is the magician's technique of mis-direction – you look at the right hand while the left deposits the rabbit in the hat. Thus, instead of answering the question, you draw attention to whatever diversion comes to mind. For example, 'Ah, yes, Mr Green. That is a fair point and I know that your department has done a brilliant job in that direction. You have made tremendous advances and I would like to discuss with you the further resources that might be required, if we are to be of real assistance.'

For the avoidance of doubt, questions should, where possible, be answered – briskly, briefly, satisfactorily and without disrupting your argument or the structure of your presentation. The above techniques are for those occasional but inevitable exceptions.

54

Closing

There is no point in opening a pitch unless you can close it in your favour. But the skill of closing is not the same as it is in the ordinary negotiating process. It differs in its possibilities, its techniques – and especially in its timing.

The happiest decisions, of course, are those which end in a close. You make your pitch, your quarry are impressed and satisfied, you all sit down at once and negotiate the details. Urgency may produce this result. Customers or clients may be in a hurry, or perhaps you have indicated that if you are to carry out the work or to produce the goods within the time required, you will need the order at once. Or perhaps you are taking the time of senior people who know that they are going to get the best deal from you: 'So we might as well save all our time and tie up the details now.'

Human beings (usually including businesspeople) always want that which they may not get: the shorter the supply, the greater the urge. You must be enthusiastic for your project, anxious to get the job, excited at the prospect of doing it, while at the same time appearing to be in short supply.

A bank manager friend once told me how to get money from a bank: 'No problem, my boy,' he said, 'Just convince the manager that you don't need it!'

A friend was after the presidency of a certain organization and took advice from a wily old politician: 'You must convince them that it would be an honour for them if you took the job,' he said. 'They must approach you, overcoming your natural reluctance and modesty!'

When you pitch, you are patently and deliberately after someone else's work. But it is not enough for you to want their custom – you must induce them to want you. The process starts before your presentational pitch – you must first have got onto the short list and into the battle – but the end of your pitch is even more crucial. The following are suggested approaches for convincing your prospective client of your worth, and speeding up the closing process:

- 'Our problem is capacity. We'd love to do the job for you, but if we are to meet your production date, we will have to start right away.'
- 'Time, that's the problem.' (Bring out your diary.) 'I'll have to do some fancy juggling, if I'm to give it the time/attention it needs.'
- 'So those are our proposals. We believe that we can provide precisely what you want, in the most cost-effective way. But we do hope that you will be able to decide very swiftly, so that we will be able to meet your deadline.'
- 'I want to supervise this job myself. I'll have to clear the decks for you. I'd appreciate the maximum warning.'

So there's the balance. On the one hand, you must not let down current customers or clients, or new ones won't want you. On the other, you must be patently in short supply in the present or you jeopardize your future. Push for a swift close, but leave yourself bargaining room, in case you have to wait.

Never forget our third question: Why? Why are you making the presentation? What do you want to get out of the presentation? Focus your mind on your target and you are far more likely to get it.

So plan the close before you open. Preparation aims at the end, from the start. You work towards the result before you reach it. Know what your clients are after; build up your confidence that you can provide it – and then transmit that confidence to your clients.

55

When It All Goes Wrong

A friend of mine, a senior executive in a major advertising agency, told me what had happened to him and to his firm, when everything went wrong with a pitch. He and his team had spent most of the previous Christmas preparing a pitch. They had produced a marvellous document, filled with excellent ideas and they were justly proud of it.

They had intended to do a dress rehearsal and run-through the night before the pitch. But a crisis arose, and the run-through was cancelled. They arrived at the pitch, breathless. They had been given one and a half hours with half an hour for discussion and questions.

As the pitch began, things started to go wrong: 'We felt it all slipping away from us, so that even as we were reading charts which were well-written and were in mid flow of a thought process which was very clear, the actual presentational skills went up the creek.

'When we reached the end of the hour and a half, our client said to us "Well, I'm afraid I'm going to have to go out for a while. You haven't even begun to talk about the guts of your presentation. You haven't even shown us the advertising you are going to do for us."

'Our client left the meeting and came back a little while later, but even then we were in terrible disarray. The meeting ran on for another couple of hours, but still we didn't finish and we knew we were done for.

'All that marvellous work . . . all those Christmas hours . . . all the resources – they were wasted, because we had not got our pitch into proper order. Which is not a good way to lose – especially when our potential client said to us, very kindly, "I think I've been very generous to you. I've given you twice the time you should have had." Which was true. . . .'

A different advertising outfit demonstrated another way to lose. They spent their Easter holidays preparing a major pitch. On the night before the great day, the team who had done the preparatory work unveiled the documents to their senior people, who said, 'That's marvellous. Exactly what we want. But you're not senior enough to do the job yourselves. We're going to take over. We shan't be needing you tomorrow.'

So they took over, flipped through the documents, spent the night learning as much as they could and arrived at the pitch, ill-prepared, tired and deserving to lose – which they did.

Afterwards, the creative director who did the pitch told me: 'Yes, we underestimated the excellence of the job that the team had done. Looking at the documents, we decided that they were not quite good enough. We thought that the weight of our seniority and the fact that we took the trouble ourselves to come would impress the clients and make up for what we wrongly regarded as the inadequacy of the work of our junior team. We were wrong. We deserved to lose, though that didn't make the loss any more palatable. . . .'

There is another reason why both these outfits lost – neither had been trained to present. Few advertising agencies or PR outfits are adequately trained: because they put other people's images on the market, they seem to assume that they do not need to have expert help in preparing, marketing and projecting their own.

Here's another failure story – this time ours. We were asked to pitch to a small but successful and growing firm of surveyors. We explained in detail how we train people.

Unfortunately, however, we had explained well, but not listened enough – the contract went to competitors. Instead of explaining so comprehensively what we were prepared to sell, we should have worked more closely with what they were prepared to buy.

If half a dozen firms compete, only one of them can win and there are no consolation prizes. The rest must content themselves with the determination to do better next time – which means learning from their own, and others', mistakes.

Part 6

THE LAW

56

Contracts

The object of a pitch is to arrive at a deal. In legal language, that means 'a contract'.

A contract is a bargain made between two or more people. It has a number of essential elements. First, there must be an unconditional offer. Second, this offer must be unconditionally accepted. Third, there must be 'consideration'. Fourth, the required formalities of the law must be complied with – and written documents may be one of these.

Generally, no formalities are required for a contract to be binding. Most contracts are as complete and binding in law if they are made orally as if every term were written in letters of gold. The exceptions are, for example: contracts of guarantee or for the transfer of an interest in land, which must be evidenced by some sufficient note or memorandum in writing, signed by the party to be charged; contracts of hire purchase, of marine or life insurance and for the transfer of shares; and contracts of apprenticeship. But a contract to buy goods or services may be made orally, so a telephone conversation is sufficient to wrap up the deal. Similarly with a contract of employment.

Where a deal has not been made or confirmed in writing, however, it may be difficult to prove its terms. One party may say that one term was agreed, the other something different. So do confirm your agreements in writing whenever you can. And do make a note or confirm anything important said to you on the telephone. Remember, if a dispute follows and reaches court, you will be allowed to refer in the witness box to notes made at the time.

It is important to distinguish an 'offer' from a mere 'invitation to treat'.

If you advertise goods, you are not necessarily bound to sell them, either at the advertised price or at all. Basically, the position is the same as when goods are on display in a shop window. They are not 'offered for sale', in the technical, legal sense: potential buyers are invited to make an offer to buy. Those offers may be either accepted or refused; or a counter-offer may be made – that is, an offer on different terms. However, failure to sell goods at the price marked on them could lead to a prosecution under the Trade Descriptions Acts.

The offer within a contract must be unconditional. If you say, 'I'll sell you these goods, provided that I've enough in stock,' you can get out of the deal if you have not enough in stock. It is not an offer capable of immediate acceptance.

The offer must also be accepted in its entirety. For instance, suppose that you offer to buy goods which you see advertised. You set out the price you are prepared to pay and the dates when you wish to have delivery and you leave no 'ifs' or 'buts'. The supplier writes back saying, 'Thank you for your letter. Your order is hereby accepted and we confirm that delivery will be made in accordance therewith.' The deal is done.

Now suppose the letter of acceptance contains, printed at the bottom or on the back, terms and conditions inconsistent with your own. In effect, the suppliers are saying 'We accept your offer – but subject to your agreeing to our terms and conditions as printed hereon'. This is not an unconditional acceptance – it is a 'counter-offer' which may be accepted or rejected by potential buyers as they see fit.

It is for this reason that you should look closely at the terms and conditions on letters or other documents of this kind. Remember that if you do nothing about them and simply accept the goods, the chances are that the counter-offer will constitute *the* offer and your acceptance of the goods will be *the* acceptance. Hence, that acceptance will be subject to the supplier's terms and conditions. An exception to this is exclusion clauses (which may not be valid if they are unreasonable). Provided that the terms and conditions are legible and not excluded by law, they constitute the terms of the contract. If people choose not to read contractual documents then, in the eyes of the law, that is their look-out

Only customers under the age of eighteen or whom the law regards as being of unsound mind may be able to avoid their contractual obligations.

Like an offer, an acceptance (if it is to conclude the bargain) must be unconditional. In English law, the third essential – 'consideration' simply means some *quid pro quo* – some return for the value or promise given, for example, 'In consideration of our paying you £ . . ., you agree to supply me with. . . .' The consideration on one side is the promise to pay the specified sum; on the other side, it is the promise to supply the goods in return for that sum.

If buyers allow individual employees to place orders on their behalf, then they are as bound by that order as if they had given it themselves. (This company has no existence in human form: someone must act *for* it. If you give someone your authority to contract on your behalf, then you are bound by the contracts made by that person pursuant to that authority.)

If you 'hold someone out' as having your authority to act on your behalf – that is if, in legal terms, you give them your 'ostensible' authority – then you are, in effect, saying to other people: 'This person is my agent, entitled to contract on my behalf.' If someone relies upon this statement, and as a result makes a contract with you, then you will be bound by that contract. You must not 'hold out' people as having authority which they do not in fact possess. If you do, you cannot expect the law to free you from deals made as a result.

A contract must not be 'too vague to be enforceable'. The law will not make contracts for businesspeople who do not bother to do so for themselves. So it is sometimes possible to avoid a contract if it can be shown that any of the essential elements of that contract are missing. For example, suppose that your customers had agreed to buy goods. The delivery date was fixed and the goods themselves were decided upon, but you left the price unfixed. Alternatively, suppose that the price was fixed but that the quantity to be taken was not. In either case, one of the essential terms of the deal would be missing. The contract would be too vague to be enforced.

In summary, if a person of full capacity makes an unconditional offer which is unconditionally accepted by some other person of full capacity and the terms of the contract are adequately set out and agreed between them – and provided that there is 'consideration' – the contract is complete. Where an agent makes the contract on behalf of his or her principal, it rarely matters whether the agent had the actual authority of the principal to contract on his or her behalf. It is enough if the agent had the principal's authority to do so. (Written authority is only necessary in exceptional cases. When required, it should always be undertaken with precision and care.)

Remember that if you tie up your deal orally, it will probably be as binding in law as if every detail was set out in writing – but it will be much more difficult to prove. If you do not get confirmation from the other party, then you must write and confirm a deal yourself. Supplement your oral agreement with writing and you not only increase your chances of victory in any dispute but, much more important, you reduce the *likelihood* of litigation.

A judge once remarked: 'As time goes on, memory fades but recollection improves.' Write while memory is fresh and you will not need to try to reconstruct.

Finally, if you convince potential clients that they should make a deal with you at the pitch itself, can they afterwards squirm out of it? Are they bound by deals made on the spur of the moment?

In a certain, limited number of cases – in particular, hire purchase or credit sales agreements made with private buyers in their own homes – the law provides for a 'cooling off period', during which the buyers can cancel. This does not apply to deals made at pitches – if all the main elements of a contract are present, the deal is done.

57

The Money You're Owed

There's little point in winning a contract unless you can enforce it. If you make your deal and the clients 'cry off' or cancel, or you carry out the services or supply the goods and they do not pay, you may need the law.

Steps before action
Litigation is a luxury and a last resort. Normal preliminaries are:
1   Submission of accounts; statements; polite reminders (oral, by all means – but confirmed in writing, especially if debtor's representative promises payment).
2   Stiff written demand; then a threat to place the matter in the hands of lawyers or a debt collecting agency.

Professional help
If your efforts to recover the money you are owed all fail, then – unless the debt is very small – you should put the matter into the hands of your solicitor. It is essential that you understand the basics of collection so that you can provide the solicitor with the information required; to issue appropriate instructions so as to ensure that you are not simply throwing good money after bad; and so that you can assess tactics together.

The alternative – which requires at least an equal amount of knowledge – is to consult professional debt collectors. The basic principles of each method are the same.

Unless you know of, or are recommended to, a thoroughly reliable debt collecting agency of excellent repute, or unless your solicitor recommends the use of such an agency, you are better off to leave the collection to your solicitor.

Legal preliminaries to action
Before starting proceedings, your solicitor will normally write a

'letter before action', informing the debtor that unless payment is made forthwith (or within such time as is stated), proceedings will commence.

If oral pressure is required – or especially if the debtors have indicated their intention to defend proceedings and have themselves appointed solicitors – direct approach (oral and/or written) will be made to them.

To sue or not to sue
Before making the final decision to sue, consider the following:

- Amount of debt. The smaller the sum the greater the temptation to write it off.
- Solvency of the debtor. Suing a man (or a company or firm) of straw is a waste of resources.
- Availability of debtors. If they have 'done a midnight flit' or gone abroad, the cost of employing process servers, enquiry agents or others to serve the writ or summons will probably mean it is not worthwhile to sue.
- Nature and strength of defence. The more real the defence and the more likely the prospect of the debtor pursuing it, the greater the incentive to compromise or (at worst) to write off.

Defences
Likely lines of defence would probably have been disclosed in the pre-litigation discussions and/or correspondence. Unfortunately, a determined debtor (or one who is fending off the day of payment as best it can – probably because of its own poor cash flow position) has many possible defences. Common examples include:

- 'No contract', that is denial of agreement to supply goods or services charged for.
- Defective goods or services: (i) breach of express term, for example goods or services not in accordance with specification or quotation, and/or (ii) breach of implied term, for example that goods will be of 'merchantable quality' and services carried out 'in a workmanlike manner and with reasonably suitable material'.

The vast majority of legal actions never reach trial. Either the defendant pays or there is a compromise. But the most unlikely defendants fight.

The cost of proceeding

Before proceedings start, you must either place a limit on the sum which you are prepared to spend in the hope of recovering the debt; or you must brace yourself to go the whole way; or you must take a preliminary view. In any event, you should ask your solicitor to estimate the cost involved.

While a business or professional person may (with allowances for contingencies) estimate with some degree of certainty the sum likely to be involved in a project, a solicitor can rarely give more than an interim and provisional estimate. The following items are seldom possible to assess precisely in advance:

1 The vigour with which the defence will be pursued and, in particular, the number and nature of interim applications or summonses – and/or the appeals which you will bear (by both sides).

2 The extent of 'discovery' – that is, the cost of inspecting and, where necessary, copying relevant documents.

3 The experience and eminence of counsel who will be employed by the debtor – and which will of itself often dictate which counsel are engaged on your behalf. (For example, will the debtor employ leading counsel?)

4 The eventual length of the trial – which will depend not only on the complexity of the issues and the extent of the dispute between the parties, but also upon the number and nature of the witnesses and upon the personality and patience of the judge.

Into the scales go all the pros and cons, and whichever course you choose – to sue or to write off – you must make your choice in full knowledge of all the facts and with your eyes wide open to the potential risks and results.

58

Libel and Slander

One danger of speaking ill of your opponents or competitors in a pitch is defamation. This is a complex area of law.

Definition
A statement is 'defamatory' if it would 'lower' the person referred to 'in the eyes of right-thinking people'. So if you call people cheats, liars or rogues; if you allege that they are bad at their business; or corrupt or negligent in their dealings – then you may have 'defamed' them.

A defamatory statement made in writing or in any other permanent form – including television or radio broadcasting – is a 'libel'. The same statement made orally is a 'slander'.

Libel is easier to prove because the evidence is on paper or on tape and (broadly) it gives the victim greater rights in more varied circumstances. If slander is proved it is usually equally 'actionable'.

'Justification'
No one is entitled to an unearned good name. So if the defamatory statement is substantially correct, then it is 'justified' and the victim will receive no damages.

If defendants plead 'justification' and fail, then they have repeated the defamation – loudly and publicly – and the damages will be multiplied.

'Fair comment'
The law generally protects people's rights to express opinions – as opposed to mis-stating facts. So you may comment on a matter of public interest, even if that comment is unfavourable to another individual or company. Even if the comment is not 'fair', that is in the sense that it goes beyond good sense and decency, this does not remove the defence. 'Mere vulgar abuse' does not constitute defamation.

'Privilege'

The law recognizes that freedom of speech must sometimes be absolute: which means in courts or in Parliament, but nowhere else.

In some circumstances, the privilege to defame may be 'qualified'. NB: the law recognizes that no businessperson is bound to provide either a trade or a personal reference, yet the giving of references is commercially necessary. Providers of references give information under a moral duty to others who have a direct interest. So the occasion is 'privileged', but subject to one qualification: if a defamatory statement is made out of 'malice', then the privilege is destroyed. ('Malice' for this purpose means any unlawful motive – in general, the wish to harm the person defamed, rather than the wish to assist the recipient.)

Defamation cases arising out of references are almost unknown. Legal aid is not available for defamation actions, and contents of references are difficult to prove. Statements made are likely to be 'justified', that is, substantially true. And anyway, 'malice' (in the legal sense) is difficult to prove.

In practice, the greatest legal danger in the giving of references comes not from defamation but from negligent actions, that is from an incorrect reference, personal or trade, given carelessly. You may avoid the peril of negligent actions by adding the magic words 'without legal responsibility' to all references. (Pleasanter wording: 'while we are pleased to provide trade-personal references, we do so without legal responsibility'.)

What, then, of words spoken in a competitive pitch? Suppose, for instance, that you run down a competitor; that your prospect passes on that news; and that you are sued. Could you successfully plead 'qualified privilege'?

So far, no court has ever had to decide – so don't be the test case. It is far safer to present your own case with maximum praise, without directly knocking your adversaries.

59

Corruption

How often have you suspected that opponents in a pitch have some improper connection with individuals doing the judging? How often have you heard that someone is getting a 'kick-back'? How often have you been asked for 'commission'?

Happily, corruption is not as rife in Britain as it is in many other parts of the world. But it is more common than most business people are prepared to recognize.

With some order books shrunken and some sellers starved for business, the temptation to tempt has never been greater. But nor have the dangers of succumbing to it, once that narrow borderline between the lawful tactic and the corrupt practice has been crossed.

So when is a gift, by whatever name, a proper oiling of the wheels of commerce – and when is it a criminal wickedness, for the actual or attempted giver or receiver alike? When does an incentive or promotion scheme, properly accounted for (and even lawfully tax-deductible) turn into an unlawful operation, which could lead anyone concerned with it – not least the executive who paves the criminal path – liable to heavy punishment?

Essentially, the difference between the proper and the criminal lies in that one word: 'Corruption'. Call it by whatever name you wish and it is still bribery. A 'backhander' by definition is not given openly and from the front – it is hidden, stealthy and corrupt.

The 'drop' occurs by stealth; so does 'dropsy'. 'Payola' is never accepted with the employer's consent.

Overseas, the 'slush' is sometimes regarded as an inevitable precursor of trade. 'Dash' is one way crookery; 'double dash' is twice as evil – involving, as it does, the repayment of part of the haul by the recipient to the donor.

'Greasing the palm' may make orders easier to slide out of the customer's hand, but it is inevitably a private gesture. In ordinary language, it is 'bribery' – in law, by whatever name, it comes within the powerful ambit of the Prevention of Corruption Acts.

Ordinary incentives are proper, accepted and lawful. Journals promote 'incentive marketing'. Business gifts, sufficiently small and duly imprinted, are tax-deductible items. Commerce and governments alike recognize the need of businesses to promote their products or services.

The limit comes when the behaviour is 'corrupt'.

Curiously, the word 'corruption' is not defined by statute. The late Lord Chief Justice Goddard once remarked that corruption is 'like a sausage – difficult to describe but easy enough to smell!' It is a secret, hidden process.

There is all the difference in the business world between making a straightforward, open gift and sliding someone a corrupt bribe. The former will be sent to the office, works, or place of business with the knowledge of its proprietors or of the recipient's employers. The employer may then require a subordinate to return the gift; or may say: 'Put it into the staff fund' or towards the Christmas bonus or celebrations. Or he or she may say: 'Keep it – you've earned it.'

If, though, the gift arrives at the employee's home – if the deed is done surreptitiously and away from the view of those who would no doubt object – then it has upon it the firm seal of corruption.

At that stage, all those involved are at risk. Parliament places precisely the same level of blame and penalty upon the givers as upon the receivers, upon those who seek to give as upon those who attempt to obtain.

You are not bound to inform the police of corruption or of any other criminal offence that comes to your attention. You are not forced to disclose (for instance) the 'fiddling' of your books by a sacked employee. You may, if you wish – for whatever reason, however altruistic or disreputable – simply remove the offender from your premises and your payroll.

This applies even to those who accept corrupt bribes from others in return for rejecting your pitches. If you can prove your suspicions are well founded, the law will not force you to hand the suspects over to justice. You may do so because you consider it right; or you may decline, because you have sympathy for the people and their predicament; or because you would rather not reveal to the world at large, or possibly even to your own colleagues, the way in which the offenders were able to get away with their impropriety for so long, through your own failures or those of others to run a tight system.

What you may not do is impede the police in the proper execution of their duties. Nor must you yourself partake in any crime, and corruption is a crime.

It is unlawful, then, corruptly and dishonestly to give or to receive, to attempt to give or to try to get a bribe, in return for some favour. Favours are inevitable: a business may give to a charity, out of kindness or goodwill, but it is not itself a charitable concern and will not make presents or present commissions otherwise than in the hope of future favours. Even if the giver recognizes past favours which the recipient was pleased to provide for no personal advantage, the element of hope for future benevolence is seldom absent.

Still, the prosecution must prove giving or receiving or the attempt to give or to get; the wish to earn a favour; and above all, and most difficult in practice, the corrupt motive. As usual, the presumption is of innocence: it is for the prosecution to prove corruption beyond all reasonable doubt.

There is, however, one massive exception to this rule. It does not apply to those who are employed by local or national government or by nationalized industries. Those who give or try to give to public servants are doubly at risk – as are those servants of the public who actually receive, or who attempt to do so. In such cases there is a presumption of corruption. It is for them to disprove dishonesty if they can – in practice, a tough task indeed.

In practice, defendants on corruption charges invariably maintain that their activities were honest and above board – that the transactions were carried out in a spirit of friendship and not of stealthy wickedness. Neither the size of the gift nor its season is a legal criterion for wrong-doing.

Do you believe that a bottle of whisky is proper but a crate criminal? Then you are in the misinformed majority. In the immortal words of a famous judge: you cannot be just a little bit corrupt any more than a woman can be a tiny bit pregnant! You either are or you are not. The size of the gift may be evidence for or against the implication of corruption but it is far from crucial.

Nor does the nature of an incentive determine its propriety. A corrupt present may be in cash or in mind – a tangible joy of food or drink or valuable gift, or the passing pleasures of yachting weekends or meals in grand style.

Finally, it is no defence for the accused to maintain that their generosity failed to achieve its desired effect. Nor will the recipient be acquitted if the bribery did not achieve its object.

These rules apply, then, whether the gift is intended to win pitches, to extract secrets before the event or to secure orders after it. The purpose of the corrupter is to induce a favour, through dishonest means. Equally, the intent of the recipient is to win corrupt benefit, in return for favours which he is in the actual or believed position to produce. Either, if convicted, may be fined or imprisoned – and in the case of public corruption, maximum penalties are usually much higher. The intent – usually successful – is to maintain an area of public integrity even higher than that in the public sector.

In practice, the authorities tend to turn a more benign eye towards corrupt practices required to achieve export orders (though they are certainly not under any legal requirement to do so). If the people bribed are outside the jurisdiction of the court, then they will receive their 'come-uppance' (if any) from those concerned with the maintenance of a decent society in their own countries. Those who bribe here — together with those professional advisers who are involved in the wrong-doing – must answer to the duly appointed investigators and courts of the United Kingdom.

The purchase of trade secrets, though, seldom requires corrupt methods. 'Leakage' is more likely through the loosened tongues of executives at leisure; by the venom of furious employees who feel they have been unfairly treated; or (and here is the top business source) by people who come for interview for equivalent posts and who are only too pleased to pass on to the interviewer what they are, or have, been up to.

If an inducement is given in return for a favour, whether by way of the revealing of information or, more likely, the giving of business, corruption is the key to criminality and secrecy the clue to corruption.

Part 7

THE FOLLOW UP AND THE END

60

Follow Up

'Don't phone me, I'll phone you.' In ordinary life, you can say goodbye to your prospects – after a pitch, be patient. When they say 'We'll let you know', they usually will.

Silence is usually bad news. If it goes on too long, follow-up time has arrived.

The most usual follow-up method is a telephone call to your top contact. Listen carefully to the reply – maybe the man who decides really is away ill; perhaps their budget for the next 12 months is indeed being revised; perhaps she is telling the truth when she says that they are still making up their minds.

If the answer is along these lines a little shove in the right direction might help. Would they like some extra documentation? Would their chairman like to have a word with yours? Apart from these gentle nudges, you will probably just have to wait, along with the other contestants.

There are two other follow-ups: when you win; and when you lose.

In most pitches, the winner takes all, and there are rarely any consolation prizes.

The top essential for losers is to find out why; to search out the reasons and then learn from them.

You may lose because the contest was rigged, fixed in advance – in which case you must shrug, walk away from your wasted resources, and hope that your presentation was so excellent that, one day, they'll come back to you. It does happen.

Too often, your judges won't tell you why you lost, so you will have to guess. Check this list:

- Did you field the right team – with the best leader?
- Were they at the level most suited to your quarry's perceptions and wishes?

- Did the individuals forming the team perform well? And did they do so as a team?
- Were the individuals and the team fully prepared? Had you sussed out who would be judging and what they wanted? And did your message suit their requirements?
- Were your documentation and visual aids as excellent as you could produce? Did you provide and explain them in the best way and at the right time?
- Did you do everything in your power to see that your products or services matched your quarry's requirements?

If the answer to all the above questions is 'yes', then you were beaten either because your competitors' products or services were better than yours or because your quarry perceived them to be. Either way, you haven't too much to learn for next time. But if the answer to one or more of those questions was 'no', then learn from your loss.

If you have won the contract, you must now be sure to satisfy your new clients, to build on your win.

Sometimes, you will only have achieved a trial run, a pilot project or a probationary period. Whatever the win, grasp it, exploit it, and extend it. Settle in with the new client or customer, whose judgment is obviously so excellent that it bodes well for your future cooperation. Now give them more than they expect from you – and keep what you have won!

61

Keep at It and Stay Young?

Why do people want to go on pitching to win? While entertaining five businesspeople, I asked them, 'If you've got plenty to live on for the rest of your days, why are you still competing for contracts, for work, for profits?'

The first replied: 'Yes, I could live on what I've saved. But not in the style to which my family and I have become accustomed! So there's no quitting. Anyway, I enjoy it. It's a sensational challenge.'

'But also the greater the risk,' I said. 'I remember when your business was doing badly. Surely you didn't sleep well at night? And it could happen again.'

'I always sleep well,' he answered. 'The bigger the problem, the greater the challenge. And in its own way, the greater the fun.'

'You're mad,' said the second. 'I can't wait to sell out and to get out. Not long ago, the business that I'd built up over 30 years nearly collapsed. The ultimate victory to me will be when I can clear out. I'll keep my fun businesses going. I wouldn't want to retire completely. But the big one? No thank you. I've seen it all before: I recognize every problem and every success.'

'I'm enjoying every minute of my work,' said a third person. 'We're building. I'm flying. It's tremendous. And I don't propose retiring, ever.'

'Never?' I queried. 'You want to go on at the same pace as you are now?'

'I didn't say that. I just want to keep on pitching.'

The fourth person had just sold his business. 'I've won for long enough,' he said. 'It was a dream. Our main competitors came to me and said: "We're either going to buy you out or we're going to open up smack in your area and in a big way." Within two days, we'd agreed a price and that was it. And am I happy!'

'Happy to be out of business?' I asked. 'Happy to do nothing?'

'Who said I'll be doing nothing? I'll take a rest and we'll see.'

Which means that he'll be out on the road again, pitching away. Winning is a habit. Once you've got into the habit of competing, the way to fend off old age is simple: keep at it, if you can.

Index

Also published by Hutchinson Business Books Limited

JANNER'S COMPLETE SPEECHMAKER

Widely acknowledged as the definitive work on the subject. Here is everything you need to know, from how to project your voice and avoid tripping over the microphone, to how to deal with the hecklers and propose a graceful vote of thanks. Also includes a comprehensive selection of draft speeches for every occasion and a much celebrated compendium of retellable tales.

ISBN 0 09 174073 8

JANNER'S COMPLETE LETTERWRITER

Firmly established as the authority on this subtle and vital art. Keep this book at hand and you will have constant access to failsafe formulas and dependable guidance for every letter you write.

ISBN 0 09 174068 1

JANNER ON PRESENTATION

Effective presentation skills make for effective management. Here, Greville Janner – one of Britain's foremost experts in business communication – demonstrates the simple but powerful techniques required for successful presentations, whether by letter, fax, telephone or meeting.

ISBN 0 09 174040 1

JANNER ON COMMUNICATION

This clear, concise but comprehensive guide shows how anyone can develop the subtle and vital art of communication. Learn how brevity, sincerity and time management can transform your dealings with all types of audience, and ease the everyday communication which is crucial to success.

ISBN 0 09 174168 8

In-company and public communication training courses and consultancy by Greville Janner and his team of consultants include: 'Beauty Contest' training; effective business presentation and speechmaking; radio and television skills; report and business writing skills; effective telephone techniques; and rehearsals and 'refreshers'.

For details, contact:
EPS, 37 Fortess Road, London, NW5 1AD
Tel: 071-267 7792   Fax: 071-267 6394

HUTCHINSON BUSINESS BOOKS

Hutchinson Business Books publish a wide variety of books covering all aspects of business and management.

If you would like to know more about Hutchinson Business Books and would like to receive a copy of our current catalogue, please write to the address below:

Please print or type clearly:

Name   : _____

Position   : _____

Company : _____

Address   : _____

_____

_____ Postcode: _____

Send to : Hutchinson Business Books, Random Century House, 20 Vauxhall Bridge Road, London, SW1V 2SA